For Laura

Simon Phipps

D0968215

Laura Dunn
'03

Simon Phipps

A Portrait

Collected by

*Caroline Gilmour and
Patricia Wyndham*

Edited by

David Machin

continuum
LONDON • NEW YORK

Continuum
The Tower Building, 11 York Road, London SE1 7NX
15 East 26th Street, New York, NY 10010

www.continuumbooks.com

First published 2003

British Library Cataloguing-in-Publication Data
A catalogue record for this book is available
from the British Library.

ISBN 0–8264–7138–2

Typeset by RefineCatch limited, Bungay, Suffolk
Printed and bound by MPG Books Ltd,
Bodmin, Cornwall

Contents

Contents

Contents

Illustrations

Introduction

Address given at the Memorial Service for Simon Phipps in Southwark Cathedral, 26 April 2001

MICHAEL ADIE

Simon Phipps sparked – perhaps sparkled is a better word – in so many different directions that we each perceive striking colours but find it hard to see the total portrait. The obituaries have spoken of him as soldier, courtier, playwright, comic actor, mimic, priest, chaplain, industrial missioner, bishop, gardener, painter, lover of poetry, counsellor and man of prayer. With so many gifts he might have dissipated his diverse energies and skills, yet he was a man of such integrity that all these skills and interests were held together in a rounded personality. And what struck those who knew him was not so much his achievements and abilities, which were diverse and sure enough, but his warm and attractive personality. He was at ease with himself and with anyone he met. He was gentle but strong; friendly although underneath quite lonely; deliciously humorous but with an underlying seriousness. He enjoyed the ludicrous, but had a sense of dignity. He had a sweetness of character without ever being sugary. He was so attentive to us that we felt taller and stronger for having met him. So rather than try to list all his abilities and achievements, we look rather for the quiet genius which held together these varied gifts.

The citation for the award of his Military Cross notes that he had already been wounded in Tunisia in 1943. Two years later he was wounded again in Italy.

> *19th April 1945*: Captain Phipps showed great heroism in action . . . tireless in his efforts to organize the Company for advance and regardless of his own personal safety . . . bringing encouragement where needed . . . It was just before the company started to advance that he was wounded, being blown up on a mine. By his . . . coolness in the face of danger he managed to keep his Company going forward. His conduct, which has been beyond all praise, has always been more than the execution of normal duty.

That determination to keep moving forward and his skill of giving encouragement where needed marked not just a distinguished military career but his life's work and ministry.

He had that gift of concentrating wholly on the person with whom he was talking, so that people felt listened to, cared for, encouraged; he gave people self-respect. But his encouragement was never bland; he always wanted people to grow and to move forward, just as he pleaded for the Church to move forward. He was so at ease with himself that he could be at ease too with royalty and equally relaxed with gauche students or working men: we were ready to confide in him and to trust him. He gave encouragement where needed.

Perhaps his most fulfilling years were in Coventry where he developed the industrial mission. Out of that experience he wrote *God on Monday*[1] in the 1960s. At the beginning of that book he writes a moving exposition of the story of Moses and the burning bush, and in doing so he seems unconsciously to reveal his own vocation:

> He was brought up in a world of privilege in the Egyptian court, separate from his own people. But one day when he had grown up he went out to his people and looked on their burdens . . . He saw an Egyptian beating a Hebrew, one of his people. A secular event in the world, an ugly incident against an ugly background of injustice, caught his eye and made him think, and made him mind . . . [He intervened] He minded enough to pursue the matter further . . . He goes away . . . and there a whole welter of experiences are churning in his mind – a sense of social responsibility, a sense of despair at those for whom he feels responsible, a realization that he has set about it wrongly – too much of the public school, paternalist do-gooder. Though he is not yet aware of it, in and through all this, pressing upon him, God is speaking, raising his awareness . . . When he turned aside (he might not have done. He was quite free), God waited to see what he would choose to do . . . God called him. And he said, 'Here am I.' God said, 'Put off your shoes, for the place is holy ground.'

---

1 Simon Phipps, *God on Monday* (London: Hodder & Stoughton, 1966).

Those words of Simon drawing out the significance of the call of Moses tell us much about Simon himself.

Simon felt he was called by God and he was convinced that this world is holy ground. One of his favourite metaphors was that we should hold up the world to the light so that we can see the watermark of God through it. Much of the book breathes the air of the 1960s, and is written against the background of large-scale heavy industries which have in great measure now disappeared, and in that particular his book is now dated. But much of what he wrote remains a call to the Church nearly 50 years on. Many of Simon's radical contemporaries went on to talk of the death of God and were so keen on relevance that they seemed almost to leave the gospel behind. Simon was deeply and surely biblical in his thinking and writing, convinced that the Christian faith and life had to be lived not just in personal and family contexts but in secular society. This world, he saw, is holy ground, the medium through which God speaks to and encounters us, and where we respond to him. So it is in the urban and industrial context that God's love must be worked out in terms of justice. Simon discerned the divine order in everyday experience. And he thought the Church had become too preoccupied with its internal life and ecclesiastical concerns. He was right then, and he is right now.

Simon became Bishop of Horsham in 1968 and then Bishop of Lincoln in 1975. They were both surprisingly rural appointments for a priest who had spent so much time in industry and broken new ground in urban and industrial mission, but then the Church of England has not always been strong on logic, and its appointment system is a touch random. Simon's pioneering spirit stayed with him in rural Lincolnshire and led him to take initiatives: local ordained ministry, women's ministry (was he the first bishop to appoint a lay woman to be in charge of a parish?). He promoted consultations between allied disciplines at Edward King House, developed a pastoral care system for the Lincoln clergy. And while doing all this he continued his interests in industrial mission and William Temple College.

Simon often said he was not a very good or successful bishop, but he was quite wrong. He meant that he did not give a clear and decisive lead to the diocese in formal terms, declaring diocesan policies or creating new structures; he was better with ideas than he was with policies or administration. He struggled to hold together a senior staff who were not all by instinct or training team operators. Looking back, perhaps it is surprising that neither he nor his colleagues tackled the agricultural industry in Lincolnshire with the same imagination with which he had tackled heavy industry in Coventry. Perhaps that was because the landed gentry of Lincolnshire could not quite understand a patrician bishop who did not socialize as his predecessor had done, and Simon probably surprised them with his liberal and left-wing views. But even if there were gaps in his episcopal ministry, his leadership and style were strikingly effective and were unconsciously taken on by those who worked with him: he would not be committee-bound, he was patient and encouraging with his own staff as individuals, he spent prime time with clergy and parishes, ensuring that they had available skilled professional care where that was needed, and his marriage to Mary, although not immediately easy, was a gain not just for Simon but for all those who worked with him. More than that, people grew in admiration and affection for a priest and bishop who was so patient with error and weakness, so devoted in prayer and discipline, so discriminating in things of beauty and elegance. He gave encouragement at every turn and made people feel they were treasured and capable of more than they had thought was in them.

One of Simon's Lincolnshire colleagues asked him about the role and purpose of a bishop. Simon responded quite readily: Resurrection. The bishop, Simon saw, is a man of reconciliation, of resurrection, giving people hope, offering the old or existing life as the material out of which God can create new life. His own work as a bishop was on those lines. He treated people as adult and responsible, and wanted them to know themselves and to be at ease with the fragility of their own personality but to recognize that out of that God could and would create new life. His own life of prayer was firm, disciplined and far-reaching (remember, a book with seventeen pages of people for whom he prayed was found after his death – he remembered us all even when we forgot him). Our many memories of him, ranging from the ridiculous (no one else could so ludicrously impersonate a pheasant crossing a road) to the devoted (someone said his address at a confirmation was the most deepening and moving they had heard) seem so fragmented and partial. But what surely God does in resurrection is to take all the bits and pieces of what we are and have been and to refashion them together into a wholeness and completion that transcends death and time. And we see through a glass darkly how God had already done that in Simon, drawing together that diversity of gifts into a rounded lovely person.

Simon was self-deprecating, almost to a fault. He told against himself how one icy Sunday morning he was driving to north Lincolnshire and listening on the car radio to the broadcast of a Lent talk which he had himself pre-recorded. He came to ice, the car skidded round, and Simon found himself facing backwards listening to himself instead of going on to Humberside. It symbolized for him the ease with which we can be knocked off course and become self-absorbed. He was self-effacing in so much of what he did, because he was able to devote himself so wholly to other people. But that was achieved at some cost. In his book he concludes in a passage which he italicized how for adults Jesus is the master-key. 'To be men of age means we are mature people to whom God has given the key to life in Jesus. Then we are on our own. But the key enables us to take full responsibility for living in the secular world, by love, at cost, in faith and hope.' Simon lived that, and in an attractive way. When George Herbert died in the seventeenth century those who knew him began to speak of him as 'little less than sainted'. Simon would be embarrassed were we to apply that phrase to him, and yet is it so far wrong? Christ, surely, enabled Simon to take full responsibility for living in the secular world, by love, at cost, in faith and hope. To that same Jesus Christ whom God raised from the dead and who has already worked with his resurrection power in Simon, we now turn as he requested when he asked for this memorial occasion, and we use the words which he asked should conclude the address, a prayer of St Augustine:

> O Lord, to be turned from you is to fall,
> To be turned to you is to rise
> And to stand in you is to abide for ever.
> Grant us all in our duties your help,

Simon Phipps

In all our perplexities your guidance,
In all our dangers your protection
And in all our sorrows your peace.
Through Jesus Christ our Lord.

1 Boyhood

Eton

DAVID FRASER

There was something remarkably consistent about Simon Phipps, something regular and in one sense predictable. By that I certainly don't mean dull or unexciting; on the contrary he was one of the least dull, the most stimulating, the most fascinating people I remember. But there was about him, at all ages and in all phases of his life, I think, a strong vein of what I can only call – inadequately – authenticity. Simon liked realism. He loathed sham. He detected and disliked the bogus or pretentious and I remember perfectly well that this characteristic, this hunger for the genuine, was very evident in the Etonian I first knew.

We were exact contemporaries, going to Eton in September 1934, and Simon's talents shone from the first day. He was always witty – rather a rare quality in a young boy – but never unkind. He was entertaining and ingenious. During one summer a young German nobleman was enrolled as a temporary master, a Baron von und zu something I've forgotten. He was a charming man, but the Nazis had come very recently to power and sentiment in England reflected the fact and disapproval of it. Before one lesson some boy chalked swastikas very ostentatiously all over the front of the master's desk, facing outwards and, of course, invisible to him. I don't think this was in the least fair: the Baron was probably very anti-Nazi. It was also bad-mannered and improper, and could lead to disciplinary measures. There was a general whispered agreement that the offensive emblems should be removed before the hour when the master would quit at the end of school and detect them, and someone muttered 'Phipps'. Simon advanced to the master's rostrum, with a perplexed expression, and delivered a prepared request for enlightenment on some point in the previous lesson. Standing there while the Baron felt for an appropriate answer Simon, with his free hand grasping a duster, erased the swastikas. It was bold, goodhearted, funny and successful and, minor though the gesture was, it epitomized Simon Phipps.

Simon liked quoting – he had a good memory and a definite love of language. From an early age he could illustrate a point in conversation, emphasize a passion, deflate a prejudice with an apt quotation, well-remembered and musically delivered. This contributed to his theatrical skill. At that time there was comparatively little theatre at Eton, but a handful of boys were natural stars and of these Simon shone. I have never seen a better Lady Macbeth: a wonderful, demanding part. Furthermore, his rather long nose and naturally austere features when composed – although they could lighten quickly when uncontrollable laughter shook him, as it often did – were somehow appropriate to the formidable and alarming spouse of the doomed king of Scots.

Simon was, therefore, a schoolboy of remarkable qualities. He was a competent, rather than outstanding, scholar and games-player, a natural entertainer with an outstanding and original sense of humour, a lover of music and a delightful companion. But he was, perhaps above all, a boy and man of absolute sincerity. Whether speaking of matters trivial or grave he told things as he believed them to be, and this was very clear. He was shrewd. All predicted for him, accurately, a shining future because he illumined every assembly, without strained effort, without the smallest touch of pomposity and always with that delightful rather thin-lipped smile, an *inward* smile, which communicated much. A whole generation that knew him well in boyhood, of which I am proud to be one, retains the memory of a uniquely lovable and gifted person: a boy, and later a man, to whom can be given, without fear of contradiction, the epithet 'unforgettable'.

A Civilized Man

JOHN BAYLEY

Phipps, I remember thinking (I was then a new boy, and lower boy, in Lyttelton's house at Eton, aged 13 or 14, and I remember having this thought in a rather awed and perhaps rather priggish way), Phipps must surely be what is meant by a civilized man; and if so he must be the first civilized man I have met around this place. My opinion of the other boys in the house, and in the school generally, was not high; and I frequently and rather despondently reflected how awful it was going to be to have to spend another three years or so in their company. How objectionable, though I hope only in a subdued way, I must myself have been; but the sight – indeed the very existence – of a Phipps (I did not know his first name in those days) restored my morale, and made me think that life, even at Eton, might after all be just worth living.

Phipps had that effect, and not on me only. His presence seemed to raise the whole tone of the establishment.

When I say I met Phipps, although he was in 'The Library' and I was a lower boy, I was proud to feel that such a meeting had indeed occurred. We had met, and again the impression had been – just as to see him afar off had made me feel 'Here is a civilized man' – that of a few moments of civility between

14

equals. I was standing respectfully in the doorway of his room, to which I had been summoned by the cry of 'Boy!' indicating that one of the great ones was in need of our services. No other lower boy appeared – no doubt they were all out playing some game or other – and Phipps looked at me in a kindly but rather doubtful way, as if fearing that I might not be up to whatever task he had in mind for me, but being too courteous to say so in so many words. 'I don't think we've met, have we?' he observed pleasantly. 'I'm Simon Phipps. And what is your name?' This casually courteous behaviour, as if to an equal, on the part of so great a man, took me quite aback. I was barely able to stutter out my name, while he listened with kindness and attention as if he had all the time in the world. Then he handed me an addressed envelope. 'I'd be so grateful if you'd slip round to Beasley-Robinson's with this', he said. 'No hurry – it's not far – you're sure you know how to get there?' Quite overwhelmed by this solicitude for my comfort and convenience, I assured him that I did know, took the envelope, and scurried off.

So he was *Simon* Phipps! How right that seemed! – Though the idea of such a great man not only having a name that seemed so absolutely right, but revealing it so easily to such an underling, still struck me with wonder.

Next term, as I recall, Phipps became Captain of the House, and the change in its atmosphere – at least where the small fry were concerned – was magical. I rather think we even acquired first names, in the manner of today, instead of being merely Brown, Jones and Smith minor. That – for those days – was itself sufficiently revolutionary. Lyttelton's, with its scarlet house flag adorned with a sinister black skull and crossbones, had the reputation of being a tough house, at least where the fags were concerned, and few days passed without one or more of us being formally and quite painfully beaten, for burning the toast, making scrambled eggs too hard or too runny, failing to fold up adequately some great man's sports attire, or – in the last resort – simply for making too much noise – 'mobbing' as it was quaintly called; though I can't myself recall ever daring to make any noise at all: the other small creatures must have made it.

The new regime did not, indeed could not, make any official changes, but it became considerate and humane: school, as it were, with a human face. I even felt quite sorry that my time as a lower boy was nearly up, so that I should not in future have any direct contact, as between master and man so to speak with Simon Phipps and his now reformed lieutenants in 'The Library'. But I recall that if a fag made a fearful mess of the scrambled eggs he was not beaten, but steered towards some other and simpler menial task where he could do less harm.

The war had now begun, and it was not long before Simon left for the army or navy: which it was I don't think I ever knew, for the next time I saw him he had become a bishop, and an admirable bishop I'm sure, just as he had been equally admirable when as a house captain he had introduced some sweetness and light into the more disagreeable aspects of our schoolboy existence.

2 The Army

Wartime Service

DAVID TUDWAY QUILTER

As our respective parents were friends before Simon and I were born, we must have been aware of each other at a very early age; and although not intimate friends at Eton, we were certainly well acquainted there, frequently passing each other in Keate's Lane during the winter half: I on my way to the rackets courts and he making for Agar's Plough or some other distant ground to play the field game, his slim frame engulfed in a long woollen scarf bearing the colours of Mr Lyttelton's house, just down the lane from mine.

We both joined the Coldstream in 1940, and a year later found ourselves in the recently formed 6th Holding Battalion at Harrow-on-the-Hill where the companies were billeted in a number of school houses. Our time there was mostly taken up with weapons-training, dreary exercises over the surrounding area and watching the wild antics of the Poles as they flew their Hurricanes in and out of Northolt aerodrome. One incident relieved the monotony of those months when the Regimental Lieutenant-Colonel, John Wynne-Finch, paid a visit to the battalion and joined us for tea in the mess. He was sitting between Simon and me when he put two teaspoonfuls of salt into his cup, mistaking it for sugar; and the expression on his face when he drank it was such that we both subsided in helpless laughter – hardly the most suitable reaction in the circumstances and not one to encourage much hope of early promotion. The adjutant, Rupert Hart-Davis, a pipe-smoking father-figure to us younger subalterns and a somewhat unlikely soldier, was also present on that occasion. He was to become known in the 1970s for publishing his correspondence with George Lyttelton, Simon's former housemaster at Eton.

I have always believed that it was at Harrow that Simon first considered going into the Church and he certainly carried these thoughts with him during the next four years of war, fighting first in North Africa, where he was wounded, and later in Italy with the 3rd Battalion, which I joined at much the same time following the landing at Salerno in September 1943.

A bout of paratyphoid, presumably contracted from drinking contaminated water during the battle of Monte Cassino, sent me back to hospital for the rest of that winter, and it was not until March 1944 that I was able to return to the battalion where I was pleased to see Simon again after so long. He was in the process of imitating Colonel Maurice Trew in bed with flu in such a remarkably accurate way that I thought I had gone into the wrong room and almost withdrew. By then appointed signal officer, Simon told me that he was the senior subaltern in the battalion, which made me the second senior and soon to become second-in-command of No. 1 Company, so we both felt we were growing up!

Simon remained battalion signal officer for seven months during 1944, commanding the platoon of 34 NCOs and Guardsmen and two other officers, Michael Kinchin-Smith and Martin Stanley. Theirs was a unique spirit, kept alive by the knowledge that successful communication across the battalion depended not only on their particular courage and expertise, but also in no small measure on the example shown by Simon with his special qualities of leadership and sense of fun. I remember the time when, at the expense of the other companies, he was persuaded by Ronnie Strutt to supply our No. 1 Company with eight telephones and attendant wires which, becoming entangled with our extensive barbed wire protection, made it almost impossible to move at night without tripping up. Much amused, Simon named us Stalag No. 1. It was at Rionero too that Simon reprimanded me for giving the Blessing at the end of a church service which I was asked to conduct for the company and at which I became hopelessly carried away.

While our different roles in the battalion kept us apart for much of the time, there was a week in July when my company shared a mess with battalion headquarters in a comfortable villa near the Castello di Broglio, owned by the Ricasoli family and situated in the hills near Siena. Being in Chianti wine country, and with no battle in progress for the time being, we could sit and tipple all day – Simon's nose becoming redder and redder as a result, with a bright blue scarf round his neck to accentuate it.

We occasionally had short periods of leave, and in September I went to Rome with Simon, prepared for seven days of sightseeing and entertainment, but it was spoilt by Simon's departure to hospital with jaundice, miserable to miss his leave and a great disappointment for me. However, we had a more successful leave together later that winter enjoying the amenities of the Villa del Ombrellino in Florence which, following a request from our Commanding Officer, 'Uncle George' Burns, had very kindly been lent to the battalion by Mrs George Keppel, complete with Selby the butler who had remained there since the outbreak of war. Our officers went on leave there in twos and threes, according to a roster, revelling in its comparative comfort and its large garden shaded by umbrella pines and cypress trees and its terrace overlooking the city. Simon describes the scene in *No Dishonourable Name*:[1]

> In summer we had dinner on this terrace. You looked
> across Florence to Roman Fiesole and the Scots Guards
> villa on its hill – east to Settignano and west, beyond Pisa,
> to the mountains of Carrara black against the sunset. By
> the time the savoury was finished the moon would be up,
> the air was heavy with the scent of orange bushes,
> lecherous frogs flopped and croaked lewdly in a pool, and
> the fireflies sparkled everywhere like sunlight on water.

It was indeed a haven of peace and relaxation, far removed from the snow-covered slit trenches in the Apennine mountains north of Florence to which we reluctantly had to return.

In early October Simon left his signal platoon to become second-in-command to Andrew Cavendish who had recently won his majority and Military Cross in rapid succession. Simon thus joined the 2nd i/c club with myself, David Helme, Richard Caroe and George Gidney sitting back at A echelon

---

1 D.C. Quilter (ed.), *No Dishonourable Name* (London: William Clowes, 1947).

with nothing better to do except to attempt to justify our existence by saying we had to go and see the CQMS, which of course deceived nobody. The valley above which we were situated was very beautiful, shining with a golden light at the sunset hour, and Simon and I usually went for a short sharp walk before lunch, he draped in a long fur coat against the cold.

In the middle of February 1945 the 2nd and 3rd Battalions came out of the mountains between Florence and Bologna and reorganized at Spoleto in the Umbrian valley. Many officers and Guardsmen came home, and the result was a merged No. 2 Battalion in which Simon was made a company commander. I think he was a little surprised at this, as he had been given no indication and had only just returned from leave in South Africa, full of stories of peaches, cream, parties and sunshine. And so began the last phase of the war in Italy, with Simon leading his company in the thick of the fighting round Lake Comacchio during the final push towards the River Po. While on a vital and hazardous reconnaissance mission he was wounded once again and was later awarded a Military Cross for his conduct during the campaign.

The next eighteen months found us in Trieste and the surrounding hills, with guard duties against any Yugoslav threat from without. This period was alleviated from time to time by short visits to the Villa Giardino Eden in Venice which, like the villa in Florence, had also been put at the battalion's disposal. A line in my diary at the time reads, somewhat obscurely, 'Venice – Aspasia Villa – hot nights – Simon Phipps – full moon' – a memory quite obliterated now after 56 years, although it seems that we had been enjoying ourselves.

Simon returned home in August 1945 for one more year of soldiering before leaving for Westcott House, Cambridge, to prepare for ordination. Robert Runcie, a fellow student, found him 'very amusing, a friend of Princess Margaret, who appeared in Footlights' smoking concerts and wrote amusing songs, like "I want to be a line or two in Crockford". Very amusing, sophisticated.' Inevitably, from that time, I saw far less of Simon as he progressed in the Church from a curacy in Huddersfield, Chaplain of Trinity College, Cambridge, Industrial Chaplain in Coventry under Bishop Cuthbert Bardsley, suffragan Bishop of Horsham and, finally, to the high office of Bishop of Lincoln. While, for some time before this, he seemed to have lost contact with a number of former friends with whom he used to associate on the social scene in London after the war, I was determined to keep in touch with him as much as circumstances and our different lives allowed, and in October 1953 he married Elizabeth and me at North Mymms in Hertfordshire, the home of our Commanding Officer in Italy, George Burns, later adding our son Simon to his long list of godchildren whom he always remembered in his prayers, and with a card at Christmas. When he was about nine I took my son Simon to stay for a night in Simon Phipps's modest council flat in Coventry, where we had an enjoyable time ending with dinner in a Chinese restaurant. When we went to look round the cathedral, Simon discovered that he had left his keys inside and we had to push his small godson through the vestry loo window so that he could get them and unlock the door.

Elizabeth and I stayed with him once at the Bishop's Palace at Lincoln, situated in the shadow of that great cathedral which we toured with Simon after breakfast, entering in a more orthodox manner than we had in Coventry, and leaving his wife Mary to practise her psychoanalytic expertise on a patient as he lay on the sofa in the drawing-room. Some years later, on the second of three visits to our home in Wells, we showed him the delights of the cathedral and the Bishop's Palace and introduced him to Alan Quilter, a very distant relation of mine who was then Headmaster of the Cathedral School and whom Simon described (much to Alan's delight when I told him) as a fine example of muscular Christianity.

By that time Mary and Simon had retired to Sussex, and not long before Mary died we spent an afternoon with them in their comfortable house in the village of Shipley, where we found them in great spirits and as happy together as they had always been. On arrival Simon embraced me and kissed me on the cheek, a welcome which astounded Elizabeth as much as myself and from which it took me a moment to recover. It was, I like to think, just a spontaneous seal of our friendship which had endured unbroken almost since our childhood; or perhaps it was merely an act of forgiveness for my indiscretion at Rionero as our battalion fought its way north across the hills and valleys of Italy, all those years ago. But whatever the reason, it is not given to every man to be kissed by a bishop, even by one who had retired, and that moment will be engraved on my mind for ever, tinged with a slight feeling of guilt that I never had the courage to return the compliment.

The Officer

ANDREW DEVONSHIRE

In Italy, under the command of George Burns, the 3rd Battalion of the Coldstream Guards was singularly fortunate in having as nice a group of officers as could be imagined. At the very top of these was Simon Phipps. Not only was he an extremely good man (in later life it was no surprise to me that he went into the Church and became a bishop), but he was both very funny and amusing. It was not for nothing that he was related to Joyce Grenfell.

He was always immensely calm and, therefore, calmed others. I remember meeting him one night in a village when we were under heavy bombardment. He seemed totally unaware of it, and we talked of mundane matters as if we had been standing in St James's Street. He was also very good at boosting morale, often by doing a double act with Tony Suffield in giving a rendition of the marvellous Marlene Dietrich song 'Lily Marlene', which the Allies successfully stole from the Germans. It became a mixture of an anthem and the battalion's signature-tune. I particularly recall one evening after we had been briefed for a night attack that was shortly to take place. Night attacks are not easy ventures and I remember, as if it was yesterday, Simon's calming, reassuring words that all would be well.

He was an immensely brave officer. I do not think he knew the meaning of the word fear, and this lack of fear was transmitted to his men.

The battalion was closely associated with South African troops and George Burns was asked to select an officer to send to South Africa for a month's relaxation. His choice fell on Simon and, though all of us would have liked to have been selected, there was no dissent that Simon was the right choice. He was a natural leader of men, who loved him and followed him with complete trust. I count myself as outstandingly lucky to have served beside him.

Signal Officer

LARCH LOYD

Early in 1943 Simon was a platoon commander in North Africa with the 3rd Battalion of the Coldstream. In the attack on the Mareth Line in March he was wounded and evacuated.

Later in 1943, after the September landing at Salerno in Italy, the 3rd Battalion had more heavy casualties. In the New Year Simon rejoined us with many others as reinforcements and what a reinforcement Simon was!

He was in command of the signal platoon which was dispersed amongst the infantry companies with some signalmen also at battalion headquarters. Simon led them admirably. The means of communication were primitive compared with what is available today. The wireless sets were massive and difficult to keep in order, whilst telephone lines laid on open ground were often broken by shell-fire. Then the intrepid signalmen would go forth in whatever were the conditions to repair and maintain communications.

Simon ensured a thoroughly dependable service from all signalmen, showing willingness and good humour. He supervised and directed things immaculately turned out, carrying an ashen walking-stick. His presence inspired confidence. When he was there things did not seem so bad as we had before thought them to be.

After seven months as the signal officer he became second-in-command of an infantry company for the advance towards Florence. In 1945, with the amalgamation of the 2nd and 3rd Battalions, the 2nd Battalion remained in Italy and the 3rd Battalion returned home. Simon stayed with the 2nd Battalion and commanded a company. As a company commander he provided the same exemplary leadership he had shown with the signal platoon. In an advance towards the River Po he was again wounded and was awarded the Military Cross for his bravery. In the words of the citation for this award 'he set an example to all by his great courage and was an inspiration to the men in his company'.

He indeed always set an example, and I think of him still as the signal officer, for he maintained those lines of useful communication throughout his life. His conversation was constant entertainment not only for its content but also because it was expressed in clear deliberate sentences brightened with laughter. Unless questioned, he never talked about himself. Other people and things around him concerned him more.

That is how I remember him: communicating helpfully as the signal officer he once was.

Gentleman

MICHAEL HOWARD

I knew Simon all too briefly. When I met him the war had just finished. The 2nd Battalion Coldstream Guards found itself north of Trieste, in principle protecting the Allied lines of supply into Austria, in practice holding on to Italian territory claimed by Tito's partisans until its destiny could be decided at a peace treaty. We briefly garrisoned the frontier town of Gorizia, before spending most of the summer in a tiny hamlet in the barren hills further south and eventually moving into Trieste itself. On rejoining the battalion as a subaltern I was allocated to No. 3 Company, and reported to the company commander, Captain Simon Phipps MC.

Simon was already a veteran, having been wounded in North Africa and served as battalion signals officer – a particularly difficult and dangerous job – for the past six months of the Italian campaign. I was under his command, alas, only for a matter of days before becoming battalion education officer. Under the circumstances I was the only officer in the battalion with a serious job to do, and as it turned out I was to find myself doing it, in one way or another, for the next 50 years. Like most of my colleagues Simon regarded it as a huge joke, but unlike some of them he was unfailingly supportive.

Simon was quite the *nicest* person I have ever met. 'Nice' is a quite inadequate word to describe him, and if there were an English equivalent of the French *gentil*, I would use it: *gentil* as in *gentilhomme*, 'gentle' as in gentleman; far more descriptive than pleasant, polite, decent, knowing how to behave. Also he was 'gay' in the true sense of the word: cheerful, funny, life-enhancing. Both qualities were stamped right through his nature, like Brighton rock. He was an excellent soldier, commanding obedience because people trusted and liked him and did not want to let him down. He also had the capacity – not unusual in the Brigade of Guards – of remaining immaculate and unruffled under the most inauspicious circumstances: one of priceless value in the horrible mess of war. Elegant and moustached, he was every inch a Guards officer. Had I been asked what he would do in peacetime, I would have said that he would probably stay on in the regiment and do very well. I certainly would not have expected him to go into the Church. But nor would I have expected it of our adjutant Mike Hollings, whose career as a Roman Catholic priest was to be no less remarkable.

Life in those drab Slovenian uplands, when all we had to think about was the date of our demobilization, might have been frustrating, but with Simon there it was continually enjoyable. And so I gather was life at Cambridge, to which Simon went on after the war. I briefly visited friends there a year or so later to find him the centre of the *jeunesse dorée*, the star of the Footlights, the quintessential debs' delight, already a dancing partner for Princess Margaret. O God, I thought, this is awful. He will make a 'good' marriage, go into the City, make pots of money, and coarsen and deteriorate like all the rest of them.

But God had other and better ideas. To my abiding regret, our paths never crossed again after Simon entered the Church, but his success there was predictable. *Gentillesse*, courage, unselfishness, even gaiety, are qualities as admirable in the Church as in the army, or indeed anywhere else, and when combined with the gift of faith they must be irresistible. I doubt whether anyone who knew Simon could ever forget him.

The Citation

The Military Cross

Captain (temporary) Simon Wilton PHIPPS (176751), Coldstream Guards

For outstanding gallantry and devotion to duty over the period under consideration. Captain Phipps has been continuously in action over a long period. Early in 1943 he was a Platoon Commander in North Africa, never missing any action in which his Company took part until he was wounded in March of that year. On his return he became Signal Officer and was unsparing in his efforts at this most important job.

Frequently in the forward positions he was an inspiration and example of the highest class to his Platoon. In September 1944, he was made second-in-command of a Company and again showed his initiative and ability, particularly in the administration and welfare of his Company.

It was particularly on 19 April 1945, after he had got command of a Company, that Captain Phipps showed great heroism in action. Late in the afternoon the Company were ordered to advance forward through the leading Companies and capture a bridge over a canal. The village and area around had been heavily shelled and bombed and was on this day being severely mortared by the Germans. The enemy were lining the far bank of the canal and also holding the bridge, with forward posts on the near side, dug in and well camouflaged. All these enemy positions overlooked No. 3 Company's position and forming-up area, so that the casualties in the Company were heavy even before the advance had started. The whole of this area was also known to be the main defensive minefield through the ARGENTA gap. Captain Phipps was tireless in his efforts to organize the Company for the advance and, regardless of his own personal safety, repeatedly visited platoons and sections himself, bringing encouragement where needed. He set an example to all by his great courage and was an inspiration to the men in his company.

It was just before the Company started to advance that Captain Phipps was wounded, being blown up on a mine. Again by his great example and coolness in the face of danger, he managed to keep his Company going forward to its objective. His conduct, which has been beyond all praise, has always been more than the execution of normal duty.

3 The Entertainer

President of the Footlights

JULIAN SLADE

When I first went up to Trinity, Cambridge, in the autumn of 1948 Simon Phipps was already something of a legend. By then he was studying for the priesthood at Westcott House, but in the Footlights, which I joined as soon as possible, he was spoken of in revered tones for the wonderful songs he was writing with Geoffrey Beaumont, at that time the Chaplain of Trinity. Geoffrey had befriended me almost immediately, as he did so many freshmen he could see were somewhat lost in the vastness of Trinity. I was very much part of his 'set', and indeed he became the most important influence in my musical life. Sometimes we used to go together to Footlights 'smokers', where he would accompany Simon Phipps in one or two of their songs by which I was bedazzled. It was there that I first heard 'Botticelli Angel' and 'Original Sin'. Of course, through Geoffrey I got to know Simon, though not all that well. He was always charming, and encouraging to me in the songs I was beginning to write myself, but at first he seemed to me unlikely both as a brilliant lyric-writer and as a budding clergy-man, with his somewhat reserved manner and smart ginger moustache. However, when he performed he was quite trans-formed, becoming whatever the material dictated.

Needless to say I was thrilled when in 1949 Simon, as President of the Footlights, invited me to appear in that year's May Week revue *Always in June*. I only made two brief appearances, one as a Devil at the end of 'Original Sin', and the other as a tongue-tied debutante, with Simon as my formidable chaperone. Although bedecked in purple satin and tiara, he insisted on keeping his moustache, saying 'it was perfectly in character'.

As well as being a memorable 'Snow Goose' in that revue, Simon also made a deep impression on me in another bird sketch as a 'Pheasant crossing the road', in which he never said or sung a word. He only had to poke his profile round the curtain, rolling one watchful beady eye, for the audience to fall about with laughter. The likeness to a wary bird was quite extraordinary.

I always kept in touch with Simon, and in 1958 my brother Adrian and I appeared with him, Geoffrey Beaumont and Ronnie Hamilton in a one-night Trinity revue. The programme included Simon singing 'Botticelli Angel', 'Original Sin' and 'Heaven', Geoffrey and Ronnie singing 'I Spy with my Little Eye Wide Open', and Adrian and myself becoming the Beverley Sisters to render a swing version of 'Nymphs and Shepherds'. Adrian has a crackly old 78 recording of this occasion, and it reminded me that there definitely is such a thing as the 'Cambridge Voice' since we all sound exactly alike!

I think of Simon with affection, and unbounded admiration. He was an exceptional man, and one of the very best lyricists of his generation.

The Songs

ADAM FERGUSSON

The key to writing any lyric, Simon said, is simplicity. A line of poetry may teem with different interpretations and clever allusions, but an audience hearing a song for the first time can only take in about one idea per line, and even that may have to be hammered home by repeating it. If half the fun is the ingenuity of the rhyme you may have to be even more sparing with the wit. Those were his guiding rules.

His reputation as a song-writer preceded him back to Cambridge when he followed Geoffrey Beaumont as Chaplain of Trinity in 1953. He had been President of the Footlights four years before. Geoffrey was also a Footlights luminary, a scintillating pianist still working on his famous jazz mass, and a hard enough act to follow. But the many undergraduates who liked to gather round the Chaplain's circle – for social far more than theological reasons – happily swopped the experience of a Beaumont thumping his piano while cigarette ash tumbled unheeded down his cassock (a spare hand waving one towards a gin bottle) for the more ascetic Phipps from whom a glass of warm college sherry was the usual hospitable offering. We drank sherry in those days.

Those of us for whom intimate revue then seemed the ultimate in theatre pounced on him. That was not hard, because as Chaplain he was keen to make availability his watchword. He jotted down in a little notebook – he must have had many notebooks – details of every undergraduate he met: their full names, their rooms, what they were reading, their interests and anything else they let slip. 'If I don't write it down, I'll only forget', he explained, anxious not to seem like a policeman, and soon he knew and remembered more about the human content of the college than anyone.

His notebook had another purpose. When the Trinity revue was looming, it began to fill up with lines for whatever sketch or song he was working up. He thought it would be fun, for example, to have four ancient Egyptians standing in frieze mode on stage. He showed me how it would start:

> When they dug us up, we created quite a stir.
> Nobody could think what on earth we were . . .
>
> They couldn't think what we were doing
> But they weren't very clever:
> You'd have thought they'd never,
> Ever, seen anybody queuing.
>
> For we're queuing for the bus to Cairo
> And though standing in the nice hot sand
> Is inclined to make us all perspire-oh
> We know it will be absolutely grand . . .
>
> Oh, there's ever such a nice oasis
> Where we always have a half-way stop

So that everyone can pop into the places
　Where everyone is sure to want to pop.
　There is all that you could possibly require-oh
　Coffee but Nefarteetee –
　All on the way to Cairo
　With Mummy and Daddy and Me!

That made three, singing line-about. There would also be a human body with an Egyptian skirt and a fox's head ('It's perfectly true / you never know who / you'll find next door to you in the queue . . .'). Simon was going to be Mummy – and on stage he would appear swathed, precariously hobbled, in a large white sheet, only his face showing and, except when he sang, his eyes shut. A week later some more verses appeared:

You're apt to get one side underdone
If you stand about sideways in the sun;
So when we get this side nicely browned
Dad counts Three – and we all turn round.

Sure enough, they would all jump revealing their other sides pale white. Simon worried for a fortnight over how to finish it. Eventually this appeared, to be sung very slowly:

So it's home in the bus from Cairo
At the end of a nice day's treat.
Mum feels she might expire-oh
And says 'pardon' when she happens to repeat.
That pyramid was more than she could bear-oh.
Dad's having gyp from his feet.

So I have to pay the pharaoh
And we've all got
   [*pause while all scratch*]
     prickly heat.

    Houses were packed to see him as a Snow Goose making fun of Peter Scott; or – because we revived another of his past, unforgettable songs for the college revues of 1954 and 1955 – wearing a halo and a long white nightshirt and carrying a small harp to sing:

    I'm a Botticelli angel, and I'm bored
    With looking quaint and faintly overawed.
      I feel so bloody silly
      Holding up my Eden Lilley[1]
    In the way that Botticelli so adored . . .

    But please, Mr Botticelli!
    Please let me have a little fun!
    Immortality is all very well I
    Admit, but I'm only 21.
    I wanna see life! I wanna go gay!
    I wanna throw ma halo and ma harp away!
    I wanna go wild and make a lot of noise,
    And dance the hokey-cokey with the Medici boys.

    There were two songs from his theological college days. One began 'I want to be a line or two in Crockford'. The other, 'Original Sin', was a classic of its kind:

---

1 The Cambridge store.

The Entertainer

What can one do that's the least bit new
That's never been done before?
Wouldn't it be nice to discover a vice
That isn't just a terrible bore?
 I long to break out and make a sortie
 Into the world and be wildly naughty . . .

I've tried them singly and mixed-up in a medley,
But those seven old sins are so absolutely deadly . . .
Oh there must be another and I just can't wait
Until I've discovered Number Eight –

Can anyone think of an original sin?
Can someone please tell me where to begin . . .?

Anger and Avarice have both been tried;
So have Gluttony, Sloth and Pride;
That only leaves us with Envy and Lust
But there *must* be something more amusing! *Really* there must!

Something with a twist that's gay and gorgeous,
Never even contemplated by the Borgias.

Of course, I suppose that I could –
Be good.

He wrote the opening chorus for the revue *This May Hurt a Little* on the harmless theme of 'H$_2$O, H$_2$O, / Water makes your garden grow' with a battery of single rhymes:

  What've we got
  That you've not got?
   Don't tell – you've got to guess what –

Take a pot shot.
Can't not spot
    What a hot tot of what we've got.

Penny in the slot
For what we've got!
      Keep quiet – it's not a lot of rot
'cos we've got
quite a lot of that
what not another soul ain't got.

And a song for the same show, to a lilting waltz, where he
appeared as a distressed debutante speculating on the future:

Won't it be heaven in heaven, heaven a heavenly time!
No need for restraint being chums with a saint
Where everything's cosy and comfy and quaint.

Won't it be heaven in heaven, heaven a heavenly time!
No one will mind if one's badly designed,
With too little in front and too much behind.

Nobody cares what anyone wears
Or minds about how you are dressed.
It's not even rude to go round in the nude –
    Oh, think of the bliss of the blest!

There'll be masses of martyrs all covered in scars
And angels with wings on like parallel bars,
And cherubim doing the chores there as chars –
    Oh, my, what a heavenly time!
I'll be there, tête-à-tête with the good and the great;

It'll be one eternal and glorious date;
And won't it be fun there! I simply can't wait!
Oh, my, what a heavenly time!

No lyrics appear at their best in print without music. To appreciate these, one must recall not only Simon's light tenor voice, his timing and the clarity of his delivery, but his wonderful range of tightly controlled facial expressions: disapproval, horror, delight, boredom, surprise – he could do them all with a lip or an eyebrow or a squint down his nose (which is why, wrapped up in a sheet as an Egyptian mummy, his face was enough to bring a house down). That talent appeared no less strongly in his revue sketches, some of them lifted to memorability on occasion by his own dead-pan performance of a leading part – his Lady Macbeth, for instance, giving her final hospitable instructions to King Duncan at Dunsinane: 'And if you want anything in the night you must use the moat. And *don't* forget to pull the drawbridge.'

But he could produce that sort of thing off his cuff. We were sitting together once at a college feast, served with something called noisette of lamb. I told him mine was barely warm. On a few seconds' reflection, he replied, 'I've a tiny tepid noisette / but it doesn't matter, does it, / 'cos I think I'm going to buzz it / at the Master.' (I can't remember how it went on, completed on a menu card now lost.)

His mind in those days, one felt, was never far away from lyrics of one kind or another. They blossomed as effortlessly at house parties across the country as in Great Court. Some tunes were his own – hummed to music students who produced the score. Others were supplied by Peter Tranchell or Geoffrey Beaumont. And though these songs were light, simple and of the Salad Days genre and era, for the generation who knew him as Chaplain they were both marvellous and memorable – the very essence of the delight of Cambridge then.

4   Ordination

Westcott House

FREDERIK VAN KRETSCHMAR

I really have only one line to contribute to this collection of thoughts written down by Simon's friends and colleagues, all of whom have better and greater claims to seeing their thoughts laid down in print.

And that line is: 'Love you Simon!'

The quirks of wartime fate brought me into the British Liberation Army in 1944, and kept me in BAOR (the British Army on the Rhine) until 1948. These years made me fall in love with the Brits as companions, and, along the road, firmly planted me in the vineyard of the C of E.

This brought me to Westcott House, and one term after my start there, in the summer of 1948, Simon also arrived. The accounts of his achievements in the serious business of the army, and the more light-hearted ones of the Footlights, had travelled ahead of him, so I felt more than a little over-awed, and hardly destined for anything more than 'collegiate' friendship.

I need not have worried: his friendliness and consideration for the stranger within the gates were immediate, laughing me out of my manifold blunders, and introducing me to people and things that mattered much to him with unlimited generosity. Over the years friendliness became close friendship that never wavered, even when our vocational careers took us along different ways, and eventually to different countries.

The arrival in his life of lovely, loving and lovable Mary only made for even stronger bonds, enjoyed during stays at each other's successive homes, and on our shared holidays in Simon's beloved Menerbes and Luberon. It was his unshakable loyalty and affection that gave such comfort, and his daily discipline of remembering all his friends from a long list in his early morning prayers became an inspiration that I have tried to hold on to in my own life.

His capacity for attracting other people's love, and his response to them, as I was able to witness in the joy with which he was greeted, whether by his neighbours to his Coventry council flat (so indomitably 'Simonish' in their slightly drab surroundings), or the French village people's impatience to welcome him and Mary back, to serve and spoil him, and confide all their family troubles and joys, as equally by the artists and expatriates in the place – to have witnessed that, what other memory and response can there be but

'Love you, Simon!'

Huddersfield Curate

LORD SAVILE

Simon Phipps came to Huddersfield as a new curate in September 1950. I had not seen him since we were both in the same house at Eton, which I left in 1936. He was younger than me. He trained for the ministry at Westcott House, Cambridge, where he came under the influence of a great principal: Ken Carey, who later became Bishop of Edinburgh.

I went to Simon's first ordination as deacon as well as his second as priest a year later in 1951. He lived with the senior curate, Ingram Cleasby, who, after leaving to become Chaplain to the Archbishop of York, Cyril Garbett, went on to become Archdeacon of Chesterfield and then Dean of Chester. Simon was lucky in having two superb vicars to serve under: Frank Woods, who came from a distinguished clerical family and who later became Archbishop of Melbourne and Primate of Australia, and then Forbes Horan, who became Bishop of Tewkesbury.

Simon soon endeared himself to all and sundry in Huddersfield and helped to increase the congregation at services in Huddersfield parish church. His sermons were full of fire and vigour with occasional wit. He was indeed a most talented person. I can remember various presentations he sometimes put on after Sunday evensong, when he used younger members to perform in roles most suited to their temperaments.

Simon was given one day off duty every week. Sometimes he came to spend the day with me at my home – and what fun the companionship was. He was my guest at the Leeds Triennial Music Festival, which he much appreciated as he was musical as well as artistic. He was a born mimic and it was very amusing to hear him impersonating his landlady-housekeeper at 50, Wentworth Street where he lived!

Simon left Huddersfield at the end of 1953 to become Chaplain of Trinity, Cambridge. He had greatly enriched the life of the parish in those three years.

5   The Trinity Years

An Entertaining Chaplin

ERIC JAMES

My first meeting with Simon was a 'providential accident'. In 1955 I was due to leave my curacy at St Stephen's, Rochester Row, Westminster, and indeed it was all arranged that I should become Chaplain of Hong Kong Cathedral. That fell through, and it was then arranged that I should be Chaplain of Lincoln Theological College; that, too, fell through! Because my lodgings in Westminster were needed for my successor, somewhat downhearted, I went to stay at the Benedictine community at St Mary's Abbey, West Malling, while I looked around for a job. Enter Simon!

He came to the Abbey on one of his regular visits for spiritual direction, to see the Abbess, the Reverend Mother, Dame Magdalen Mary OSB, and asked her whether she knew anyone who might be suitable to be a chaplain of Trinity with him. She told him he could do worse than see the young man without a job in the guest house.

It says something about Simon that he had been able to persuade the College Council at Trinity that a second chaplain was needed. It says something more that he was able to persuade the Council that that second chaplain should be someone who had neither been to Cambridge University, nor to a public school, and who had left grammar school at the age of 14.

When, in September 1955, I became chaplain, Simon insisted I should not be called Assistant Chaplain, but that we should be as equal as possible. He allocated half the 300 freshmen to my pastoral care. He had A to K, and I had L to Z, and – just to confuse the issue – I had all who lived in Whewell's Court, where my rooms were, and he had all who lived in Bishop's Hostel, where his rooms were.

It was clear from the start that Simon's way of 'dealing with' freshmen would be very different from mine. Most evenings he would hold a sherry party for a dozen or more undergraduates, and after an hour or so would remember all their details. He could concentrate totally on the person he was with at a party. Of course, he was very practised at it, whereas I was virtually new to the game. So I saw all 'my' freshmen at half-hour intervals – ten a day.

With pastoral care went prayer. What astonished me immediately was Simon's spiritual discipline. I was never able to discover *when* he got to chapel of a morning, but it was always earlier than I did. (And I was there for 7 a.m. meditation and 7.30 matins.) No matter what time Simon got to bed, he was kneeling bolt upright at his prayer desk in chapel next morning – like a guardsman on duty. His spirituality was at first a 'threat'; I admired it – perhaps too much – but couldn't copy it.

By the end of that first term I was exhausted and wanted only to be left alone; but Simon insisted I should come and stay a few days with him and his parents at their home at Longparish near Andover. Immediately it was clear that what was completely natural to Simon was utterly exceptional to me. The first evening we dressed for a fairly formal dinner. But dinner was after 'having a few friends in to meet you' – an hour and a half's drinks party. Next day Simon suddenly had to go up to London, and I was left to go for a long walk with General Sir Richard O'Connor, Simon's uncle, who was also staying in the house (and to whom Simon had been ADC when he was GOC-in-C Northwestern Army, India in 1945). In the middle of our walk, Sir Richard suddenly turned to me and said, 'Why ever do you think Simon got ordained? He had the greatest potential as a soldier of any man I'd ever known.' Curiously, as we'd driven down from Cambridge, I'd asked Simon that very question and he'd replied immediately: 'Because I'd loved being a soldier and being a priest was like being a soldier – only more so. I could care for a wider range of people as a priest.' Sir Richard was completely satisfied when I passed on Simon's reply to him. 'Good for him!' he said.

Simon was marvellous at helping me into my job. And after having been chaplain to the whole college, it must have been quite demanding to yield part of it to another totally inexperienced at chaplaincy. We soon became close friends. In our three years together we never exchanged a harsh word.

I never felt that he had an obvious and overt 'Educating Eric' policy; but, just as he had shared his Gentleman-Usher-in-Ordinary-to-the-Queen father, and his General uncle with me, so he shared occasions which he might have so easily claimed as his own. At the beginning of my second term, Dr Billy Graham was conducting a mission to the university at the University Church, Great St Mary's. Simon simply said to me, 'I'd be glad if you'd have Billy to lunch in your rooms', and added, 'with Mervyn and John and Harry and me'![1] I'd never 'given' a lunch party before – certainly not a lunch party like that!

Simon was himself a genius at entertaining. He 'made' occasions in his uniquely elegant rooms; and you never quite knew whom you'd be meeting in them – William Douglas Home, the playwright; Mark Bonham-Carter, the politician . . .

One morning the phone rang. It was Simon. 'Eric, can you come to dinner tonight? I've got Charles Raven coming – and Mervyn and Owen Chadwick and Roland Walls. We shall all go, after dinner, to the Union, to hear Charles speak . . . But there's a word of warning: You mustn't laugh if Charles says, "I wish I could transport you all to the great green strip of the Jumna Valley." ' That seemed highly unlikely, but Simon didn't explain that he had issued this warning to all he had invited. When his doorbell rang that evening, Simon, Mervyn, Roland and I all went to the door to greet Charles and Owen. But there was nearly an explosion when Charles Raven flung his arms wide and exclaimed, 'How I wish I could transport you all . . .'

But that was not all. After dinner we all went over to the Union. Owen Chadwick occupied the chair at what was the annual meeting of the Cambridge Mission to Delhi, with Charles on his right. After Owen had introduced Charles, he flung wide his arms to the audience, and began his address:

---

1 The Revd Mervyn Stockwood: then Vicar of the University Church, later Bishop of Southwark; John Burnaby: Regius Professor of Divinity and Dean of Chapel, Trinity College; the Revd Harry Williams: later Fellow and Dean of Chapel, Trinity College.

'O how I wish I could . . .' Roland Walls dived for the floor, convulsed in hysterical laughter.

Some of the happiest days with Simon were spent together at the Trinity College Mission in Camberwell, with groups of undergraduates whom we took down in the summer and Christmas vacations. The Vicar of St George's, Camberwell and warden of the College Mission was Geoffrey Beaumont, a unique priest, who had himself been Chaplain of Trinity from 1947–52, and whom I'd first met when he was a chaplain to the Royal Marines during the war, and whom I would succeed at Camberwell in 1959. Besides undertaking edifying tasks, those of us who came to Camberwell from Cambridge would prepare an entertainment to be given in the Mission at the end of the visit – a sort of 'Footlights in Camberwell'. Geoffrey – who had recently composed his jazz mass – would accompany Simon at the piano in, of course, songs like the 'Botticelli Angel'. Afterwards, we would proceed syncopatedly (i.e. unsteadily) from bar to bar around the pubs of the parish.

One thing was certain: Simon was a detailed and diligent pastor to undergraduates whatever their background: grammar school or public school. That was confirmed in Camberwell with the mixed bag of undergraduates who would make up the party which visited the Mission. But you also saw how good a pastor Simon was with the people of inner-city Camberwell, when you might have assumed he would best be a pastor to, say, Chelsea.

Before he left Trinity in 1958, Simon spent one long vacation working in the car industry in Coventry. It made a great impression in the college that he should do this – a great testimony to the truth that he believed about 'God on Monday', and about theology and industry. And yet, perhaps, not as much of an impression as one might have imagined, because paradoxically people – dons and undergraduates – were apt to think of Simon as 'special' and 'a man apart' (an understanding of him somewhat contradicted by his Footlights gifts).

Simon was not a great preacher, but he was always a thoughtful one. He preferred to communicate what he believed in one-to-one confirmation classes and 'refresher classes' to those who wanted to 'think again'. He loved hosting in his rooms informal lectures by dons: G.M. Trevelyan on 'History and literature', Martin Ryle on 'Astronomy', Otto Frisch on 'Los Alamos' and so on.

I had gradually to face the fact that, despite all his gifts – maybe because of them – and in spite of all his friends, there was a profound and enduring loneliness to him. Simon, like Dag Hammarskjöld, would have had to say, till many years later he met Mary: 'the same continuing loneliness'. And his figure, kneeling upright in chapel in the early morning, will always speak to me of one who knew in his deep heart's core that

> The longest journey
> Is the journey inwards.

One more grateful remembrance of Simon. When he left Trinity in 1959 he gave me as a present *The Letters of John Keats*. He underlined one particular passage – on the poetical character:

When I am in a room with People, if ever I am free from speculating on creations of my own brain, then not myself

goes home to myself, but the identity of every one in the
room begins so to press upon me that I am in a very little
time annihilated . . .

This profound passage – it seems to me – sums up much of
what was Simon's ideal for himself – and what was at the heart
of how many of us experienced him.

Chaplain of Trinity

DEREK HAYWARD

In August 1953 when I was nearly 30 I came home from Calcutta, where I had been running the family business, in order to offer myself for ordination. I went straight from the airport to Cambridge and by great good fortune was offered a place at Trinity to read the three-year theology tripos. As there were still three or four weeks until term started I went up to Scotland, where I had an invitation to shoot with an old friend with whom I had served in the war. Most of the house party were also old friends who were intrigued by my change of direction, and when I said that Simon was to be Chaplain of Trinity next term, several of them said how lucky the Church of England was to have him, and my host said that he (Simon) was staying nearby for the Angus Ball in September, so that I would probably have a chance to meet him then.

We duly went to the ball, but I and the other members of the house party were so busy dancing reels (which most of us were not very good at) that I didn't manage to meet up with Simon, who was likewise engaged. I did, however, have a good look at his house party, nearly all of whom were in Highland dress, which to my ideas at the time seemed totally inappropriate for a chaplain. I decided that Simon must be the one person in a black tailcoat, who was rather a little man, as indeed am I. The only alternative was a tall handsome man in a kilt, with a somewhat beaky nose, who was dancing reels as though he'd danced them all his life (which he had), and I decided that couldn't possibly be him.

I arrived at Cambridge a fortnight or so later, and as soon as I could went to call on the Chaplain, expecting to meet the little man whom I'd seen at the ball, but to my surprise he turned out to be the tall handsome one, though he had changed out of his kilt and was now very recognizably a clergyman. We quickly made friends and found that we had quite a lot in common, and had actually both been wounded in Italy in the last month of the war, both for the second time. We had also been in the same hospital in Pesaro (an old lunatic asylum!) although we didn't meet at the time, as he had been there some time before I arrived and recovered before I did.

The men who had been in the war had all gone down by 1953 (Simon himself had gone down in 1949) so I was rather an odd fish, and though I did make a great number of lasting friendships among the other undergraduates, it was a great joy to me to find such a kindred spirit as Simon. Although he had already been ordained for four years he had not read theology as an undergraduate, and had, so to speak, majored on the Footlights, with the history tripos taking something of a back seat. As my own theological knowledge increased, he never treated me as anything other than an equal, and almost deferred to me on occasions.

He was a wonderfully popular chaplain in the college, and not only with the public school men, though since nearly everyone had done their National Service they were more mature than they would have been before the war, or than they would be now, which in fact made it much easier for me, as an older man, to fit in. One of the Trinity men had suffered a personal tragedy during the long vacation and Simon was very concerned about him; as he was one of the few with whom I had some previous contact I was able to be of some use to him.

His Footlights expertise was soon called upon, and as I also had some little amateur acting experience we both took part in the Trinity revues of 1953 and 1954, when he revived some of his successes, notably 'Can't Anyone Think of an Original Sin?', 'We're Queuing for the Bus to Cairo', and the immortal 'I'm a Botticelli Angel and I'm Bored'. He and I took part in one or two sketches written by Adam Fergusson. Simon asked me to stay with his parents in Gloucestershire that Christmas vacation, and I enjoyed meeting them not long before they moved to Spain, where some years later I called on them.

One spends one's first two years at Cambridge in digs – at least that was then the custom at Trinity – and one's last in College, so in 1955 I moved into Great Court with rooms very close to Simon's in Bishop's Hostel. He very kindly suggested that I should have breakfast with him every day. As the terms were only eight weeks and a few days, this was not too great a hardship for him, while for me it was a great pleasure which contributed very largely to my enjoyment of my last year. Years later at the General Synod when Simon was retiring as Bishop of Lincoln, the Archbishop asked me if I could give him a story about Simon, so I told him that after our final breakfast Simon said to me, 'Did anyone ever tell you that your jaw creaks?' He used this to illustrate Simon's great restraint and forbearance in waiting a whole year to say it!

We got on so well that we decided to go to Spain and Portugal together in my car during the long vacation of 1956. We did this very much on a shoestring, sleeping by the side of the road when we were short of a bed for the night. We had a very interesting experience in Burgos where we were fascinated by the cathedral: as we discussed it, a very educated English voice picked up our conversation and said, 'It is rather extraordinary, isn't it?' and we turned to find a Carthusian monk standing behind us. It turned out that he had been in the Spanish embassy in London in the 1920s and knew the Prince of Wales and many others very well. He had subsequently had a late vocation and joined the order, which made him bursar – which explained why he was allowed to talk. Simon and he discovered a mutual friend or two, and then he took us round the monastery and introduced us to one of the monks.

After that we stayed with Geoffrey Beaumont, who had been Chaplain of Trinity before Simon and who was now chaplain in Madrid, and saw a side of Spanish life which it would have been difficult to find with anyone else. I particularly remember that Geoffrey had 'sitting-room gin' and 'bathroom gin', the former being in a Gordon's bottle and the latter in a large carboy. Guests were not supposed to know that the carboy was used to fill up the bottle when required!

From Madrid we drove through Spain to Lisbon, and I used to have a photograph of Simon standing in the middle of the Roman theatre in Merida declaiming 'Friends, Romans, countrymen' in order to demonstrate the excellence of the acoustics. In Oporto we managed to stay with one of the Symingtons of Port fame, because he and Simon had some mutual friend. I say 'stay with', but actually we slept under one of the trees in their drive. As an ordinand-to-be I was very impressed with the way that Simon said his Office every morning and evening throughout the trip, illustrating very well the disciplined side of his priestly life.

And so back to Cambridge and work, and as I then moved on to Westcott House I soon did not see much of Simon, though we always remained friends. I last saw him at a party some friends had organized for me, when he made a speech in verse recalling our breakfasts. He died a week later. He will remain for ever one of the great influences on my life.

6   Industrial Chaplain

Cathedral and Industry

EDWARD H. PATEY

It was in the autumn of 1957 that I received an unexpected letter from Simon Phipps, who at that time was Chaplain of Trinity College, Cambridge. He wrote to tell me that he had recently met Cuthbert Bardsley, Bishop of Coventry, who told him that the construction work on the new cathedral had now begun and that he was looking to appoint a small team to begin planning the ministry, worship, mission and staff structure in preparation for the consecration in 1962. Simon's letter to me ended with a typical Phippsism: 'The Holy Spirit is pouring lots of people into Coventry, I hope he will pour you there too.'

Early in 1958 the Bishop had made the initial appointments. Simon and I were members of the team which in due course would be joined by such specialists as the organist and director of music, the pastor to the congregation, the diocesan missioner, the youth officers and the director of drama. We met very frequently as a team for prayer, bible study and for the task of planning ahead for the future life and work of Sir Basil Spence's exciting design, due to be finished in four years' time. It was a great adventure. Simon, who was also appointed as the Industrial Chaplain, made a highly individual contribution to these proceedings with his wit, wisdom and deep unobtrusive spirituality.

Although we became a closely knit team and came to trust and respect one another, there were inevitably personal differences between us which had to be honestly resolved. In his book *Twentieth-Century Cathedral,* Provost Williams observed that the tensions between what is traditional and what is new could not be easily resolved in a place as flexible as Coventry Cathedral. The Provost was concerned that we should deliberately break new ground and not just imitate what he considered to be the outdated style of many of the older cathedrals. On the other hand the Precentor, who had held a similar office in Canterbury, was insistent that we should not neglect the wonderful heritage in liturgy, music and style simply for the sake of innovation. More than any of us it was Simon who with his wit and insight was able to break the deadlock which was threatening to disrupt our common purpose.

Simon had a great gift of mimicry and enjoyed entertaining us with brilliant impressions of his friends, colleagues and clergy. His humour was cunningly accurate, but never unkind or cruel. It added greatly to the fun of our life together in Coventry. We came to see how he made such a 'hit' as a member of the Cambridge Footlights. He gained equal enjoyment when we did our best (less successfully) to make jokes at his expense. I am told by some of his friends that years later, when he was thinking back to his Coventry days, he remembered that I teased him about the way that, when he pronounced the word 'cross', he said 'crorss', and how that made us aware of a faint whiff of *The Tatler* wafting through the Cathedral!

For the ten years that he worked in Coventry Simon lived in a small council flat in a new housing estate on the outskirts of the then rapidly expanding city. It was there that he entertained his long-time friend Princess Margaret, to the great interest of his neighbours. He did not speak much about his private life, but the rumour went around that he himself had cooked the lunch for his royal guest. During his time in Coventry he continued the discipline of a cold bath every morning. He mentioned this experience in an article written for the first issue of *The Cathedral Review* in December 1960. He said that his 'strange habit' dated back to his days as a curate when there was no hot water in his digs in the morning:

> I am beginning to wonder whether increasing spiritual maturity – a polite name for my approaching middle age – suggests otherwise. This wretched creature, stripped and shivering on the cork mat in the unheated council bathroom. The former tenant's wallpaper highlights the horror with a sky-blue background and a design of *fish*. Yes: this is the real me – naked to the world, bereft of illusions, even the pyjamas cooling now on the cold linoleum. Dear readers, how do your ideas about yourselves stand up to this moment of truth? Catching sight of yourself at this crisis in some remorseless mirror, do you really see there the popular secretary of the bowls club or the reliable father of six, you know yourself to be? How can human self-confidence possibly bear this almost indecent self-exposure. What would the chaps think if they could see one now?

His articles which appeared regularly in the *Review* were both enjoyable and thought-provoking, as was his preaching. As in his Cambridge ministry to undergraduates, so the people of Coventry warmed to his humour, honesty and friendship and soon sensed his care for everyone he encountered. The constant theme running through his preaching and writing in those years was to impress the need for a positive attitude toward change. This was particularly relevant to the people of Coventry. It was not only the ruined cathedral which was being rebuilt to a totally new design. The city centre had been redesigned in a style strongly contrasting with the old medieval city. Much of the old was being swept away, and incomers were producing a great increase in population. Many of the older inhabitants were not certain that they liked what was going on. Simon faced this problem head-on in an article in *The Cathedral Review* (December 1961):

> The other day I had a terrible shock. I bought a tube of that toothpaste which I had used ever since I can remember. I opened the familiar box and horror . . .! *They had changed the tube!* The shock sustained by the TUC at the announcement of the pay pause without prior consultation was as nothing to that which shook me as I gazed at the new tube with its streamlined *red* cap, where the erstwhile sensible *blue* one used to be.
>
> The harsh experience of a world around us – changing as we watch it – is perhaps the hall-mark of our times. A huddle of medieval buildings at some corner will suddenly disappear and up shoots a concrete framework faster than the bulbs in spring. And one finds a mixture of

reactions going on inside oneself, a sense of irreplaceable loss combined with an exciting sense of necessity and new beginnings.

It is important for Christian men and women to take all this to heart, because as far as one can see the world is never *not* going to be like this. It just is, and will continue to be one of the facts of life. For our technological resources are developing faster and faster, giving us an increasing mastery over our physical conditions, so that we can change things almost overnight. New sources of power or new ways of tapping old ones, new synthetic materials, new methods of dealing with information and making it productive; all these and more are causing yearly revolutions in science and industry. This in turn is increasingly shaking up established patterns of trade and employment. Since research and technology will develop rather than retract, change is here to stay.

If the Church can stimulate industry to take this sort of thing seriously, it may bring society as a whole to a new way into the riches of Christian insight, and not least to that basic truth that balances up the rigours of change – that the God who speaks through change does not change Himself, so that we may have faith and hope because we can depend on love.

It was far-seeing of Bishop Bardsley to appoint Simon Phipps to the double chaplaincy to Cathedral and Industry. He took up both tasks with equal commitment. It would be argued that in a cathedral city with heavy manufacturing the workers on the shop-floor would mostly know very little about what goes on in the cathedral, and that the worshippers in the cathedral would mostly have little understanding of industrial life. On the shop-floor Simon was able to show the human face of a cathedral and in the cathedral he would show the human face of industry. In this way Simon made a tremendous contribution to the cathedral by helping to place it in a secular context. He enabled Church–Industry relationships to become an essential part of the cathedral's much-publicized message of reconciliation.

When he had completed his first five years in Coventry Simon wrote a report on his industrial chaplaincy for the benefit of the Cathedral Council. He particularly wanted to make the parameters of his work quite clear. He did not see it as a personal pastoral ministry to individuals in trouble in the factory. It was not an extension of the parish. It was a 'prophetic' ministry within industry itself, an attempt by the Church to make some sort of analysis of the situation of industry and the salient issues that arise within it, in order to think out what may be the contribution of Christian thought and action on those issues. This is done in the conviction that thinking inspired by the Holy Spirit of God can penetrate more deeply than any other to the real significance of human situations.

He outlined three ways necessary to undertake this ministry:

1. We have to make contact with these situations, and spend much time in learning what they are and why. We go into a factory as learners and try to learn all we can about it and its human, social and technical effects.
2. We try to learn to apply the insights of Christian thinking to the secular situations we learn about. What does a Christian

make of all this, and do as a result? Since this sort of socio-theological thinking has not been largely done since the Middle Ages, this is slow, pioneering work.

3. We seek to share our thinking with those involved in industry. This is done in constant conversation with men and women at all levels; in groups that gather at work breaks among the machines and in weekend conferences to which all major firms send management and trade union representatives.

On 27 May 1962, only two weeks after the consecration, the cathedral was filled with men and women from the industrial and commercial life of the city. Simon preached on the text 'Among you whoever wants to be great must be your servant and whoever wants to be first must be the willing slave of all – like the Son of Man who did not come to be served but to serve' (Matthew 20.26–8). When the sermon came to be printed he gave it the title 'Mastery or Service'.

> I know full well what a lot many of you do in management and unions about all this. But you know full well that industrial relations are at the mercy of economic circumstances. You are pushed and pressed by forces far bigger than yourselves. Trust is not easy to come by, not easily kept. It does and will break down. But if you are going to claim the name of Christian, you have still got Christ's word. *Breakdown or no breakdown*, not *Mastery* but *Service*.

He concluded the address with paragraphs which sum up his teaching as an industrial chaplain:

This means that when things do go wrong, you will never relax into hopelessness or cynicism. You will mind passionately that there has been a failure to follow Christ's word. And you will ask passionately what can have caused it in the past or in the present, and what can be done about it in the future. You will never accept the battle for Mastery as the final state of things.

In a nutshell, I believe employers and managers need to take the past more seriously than they sometimes do. They are challenged by the past. I believe trade unions need to take the future more seriously than they sometimes do. They are challenged by the future.

Employers cannot expect their work people to take the future seriously, with its immense technological challenges, unless they themselves take the past seriously with its immense social challenges.

If we claim to be Christians we cannot dismiss all this as impractical nonsense. We will take it seriously and press and press towards it through every failure and disappointment and mistake and through a lifetime. And we will do this because we believe deeply, deeply, that Christ never speaks a word which He will not help us to follow, and that through lives committed to Him, He can slowly change for the better the structures of industry and commerce – through that minority of righteous men and women who care, and believe and act and are ready to follow the Son of Man who did not come to be served but to serve and surrender His life as a ransom for many.

The Coventry Years

JOHN ATHERTON

Fortunately, there are a great variety of ways of meeting people which symbolize richer and more substantial relationships. For the memorable wartime classic film *Brief Encounter* that opportunity for meeting was provided by a busy, smoke-filled station buffet bar. For me, encountering Simon Phipps occurred through three equally mundane locations, which illustrated great and small things about his life. The first was through a book written in Coventry, the second a room in the Manchester Business School and the third in the lounge of Edward King House in Lincoln. They are of particular significance for me because they continue to influence me to this day, not least because they all resonate with today's greatly changed and changing world. That continuing freshness says something rather important about the nature of Simon Phipps's influence, even if through such brief encounters.

Take a book he wrote whilst Industrial Chaplain in Coventry in the 1960s. My life was first touched by Simon by reading his *God on Monday* as a young industrial chaplain in the late 1960s. It is only a little book, but I have just reread it, and it still speaks to my condition, even 40 years later in such a greatly changed context. It is a book about taking the secular world seriously, in all its different aspects, from industry to health-care, from education to social services, from employers to trade unionists, from individuals to organizations – all part of God's world, just as the Church is – a world through which we respond to each other and to God. It is a book written out of his experiences of the late 1950s and 1960s, of his deep involvement as an industrial chaplain based at Coventry Cathedral, a life of visiting the great manufacturing plants (now mostly gone), of trade unionists and managers, of totally secular agendas which men and women pursued, and which, for him, revealed deep ethical concerns and so thereby embodied God's purposes. Simon was then one of the second-generation pioneers of industrial mission, a radical ministry inaugurated by Bishop Leslie Hunter of Sheffield and his inspired choice of Ted Wickham (later Bishop of Middleton) as leader. It was Ted who taught Simon so much about industry, mission and theology, and so much about the central role of the laity in God's purposes. As the second generation of industrial chaplains, Simon therefore stood high with such British contemporaries as Bill Wright of Teeside, Richard Taylor of Scunthorpe, Frank Scuffham of Corby and Brian Cordingley of Manchester, and with such international figures as Horst Symanowski in West Germany and George Velten in France. Yet the little book showed me so much more. For Simon's initial personal impact could be deceptive. He could come across as rather reticent, overshadowed by more extrovert industrial missioners and theologians. Yet *God on Monday* reveals a Simon very aware of the very latest developments in theology, a Simon intelligent, creative and displaying a rich breadth of knowledge and experience. He was truly an interdisciplinary thinker, bringing together a wealth of fresh insights from, for example, nineteenth- and twentieth-century literature and art.

My second encounter with Simon was through the William Temple Foundation, initially based in Rugby, where he came under the influence of its redoubtable principal, Mollie Batten, powerfully symbolic of Simon's deep commitment to lay skills and ministry, and therefore particularly of the contribution of women. (Mollie was slightly unusual, combining formidable secular and academic experience with revealing baggy drawers and smoking a pipe!) He was light years ahead of most Church leaders in all these critical areas. When the William Temple Foundation moved to Manchester, to a base in the new Manchester Business School, Simon soon joined its governing council, as I did in 1974 with David Jenkins. It provided a perfect base for him, representing that great tradition of relating faith and society, resurrected by F.D. Maurice in the mid-nineteenth century and carried on in the tradition first by Bishop Charles Gore and then so splendidly by Archbishop William Temple. It was, and still is, a tradition committed to promoting God's kingdom through God's world. He became its chair until 1988. In this context I saw a Simon who carefully, but in a no-nonsense way, guided us through complex and sometimes heated agendas, always available to the staff, always prepared to listen to the elaboration of practical and theological problems, always supportive. It generated what he was so particularly interested in: a network of like-minded laity and clergy, all with great skills and experience, all committed to relating faith and contemporary society for their mutual benefit. And, in the manner of *God on Monday*, the Foundation still continues as a viable innovatory institution, now addressing the global issue of marginalization from its base in the north-west of England.

Finally, I encountered Simon in the sitting-room of Edward King House, which he so often used in the excercise of his influence as Bishop of Lincoln. The meetings to which I am particularly referring emerged from his influential role as chair of the Industrial and Economic Affairs Committee of the national Board of Social Responsibility of the Church of England, again in the 1980s. These were glorious years of a strong national Church which engaged in a very organized way with national public life. Sadly, the Church is now dismantling these bodies – another sign of its increasing irrelevance in British society. What Simon did was to use his great influence and wealth of contacts throughout national life to attract leaders in all walks of life to meet together to pursue the ethical implications of contemporary life, which he saw so clearly as *disclosure* moments of God's deeper purposes (a phrase he adopted from one of his heroes, Bishop Ian Ramsey, a distinguished theologian and philosopher and a predecessor as chair of the William Temple Foundation). I served on the Industrial and Economic Affairs Committee at the same time as Simon, and was invited to one such weekend at Edward King House. It was a delightful location, grand in an unpretentious way – a bit like Simon because of his natural ability to preside over such occasions with effortless grace. He left his mark even on what we had for breakfast – honey on freshly baked croissants. Of course, being such a quietly commanding host was made much easier for him because of Mary, his wife's influence. She was the perfect complement for him, embodying so much of what he so passionately believed in: the central role of the laity, of secular professions and skills, of a deeply religious non-religiosity, of a deeply church non-churchiosity. The weekend I am thinking of took place in 1985, and was of particular importance in my life. Simon asked me to produce a paper on the strengths and limitations of the market economy from a theological point of view, as a response to a paper also presented at the meeting by Ralph (now Lord) Harris, then the influential leader of the Institute of Economic Affairs, the foremost Thatcherite think-tank. It was the year of the publication of the influential and radical Church report *Faith in the City*,[1] in which I had been involved as a consultant. Simon, with unerring accuracy, sensed the great changes that the early 1980s heralded, from the corporate welfare society of Butskellism (linking the left of the Conservative Party under Butler, and the right of the Labour Party under Gaitskell, a postwar liberal consensus to which Simon was deeply sympathetic) to a much more market-oriented society, a consensus which I call Blatcherism, initiated by Thatcher and then continued by Blair.

Simon spotted that dramatic change in its earlier stages, unlike most other Church leaders, and so brought together the intellectual influences of the New Right and of the mainstream liberal tradition. From that organized encounter with change, I learned, for example, to take economics and market economies seriously as partial intimations of God's purposes for human living in the world, and not as embodiments of an evil capitalism. That was a great change for me to undergo – a case of changing a tradition in order to engage better with a changing

---

1 London: Church House, 1985.

context. But that of course was, and is, precisely the message of Simon's little book *God on Monday*: the lesson of reading signs of God's changing world and so responding more effectively to them. It is a reminder to me that brief encounters with Simon Phipps stay with you for ever and change you for ever.

7 The Bishop

Bishop of Horsham (1)

PETER HORDERN

The first time I met Simon was when he became Bishop of Horsham. He came to Fittleworth, near Petworth, to preach his first sermon, and I was lucky enough to hear it. The theme of his address was that 95 per cent of the world's population owned 5 per cent of the world's wealth and 5 per cent of the population owned 95 per cent of the world's wealth. He said this was unacceptable. Since his congregation was certainly in the fortunate 5 per cent, this was a brave point to make. Perhaps they did not fully grasp the point, for after the service he was surrounded by well-wishers who told him what a beautiful sermon he had preached. It was a beautiful sermon but it was also very brave.

Courage was certainly one of his qualities. But I think of *caritas*, loving-kindness, which he was able to communicate, not so much by what he said but by the way he listened with his whole attention and interested affection. He was especially good with young people. How we laughed together when he and Mary joined us for lunch or supper! It was quite infectious as one story led to another, the children beside themselves with laughter and pleasure.

I remember meeting him and Mary at an abbey in Provence

before they joined us for lunch at the house in which we were staying. To be in his company while we marvelled at the beauty of a ruined Romanesque abbey was a moving experience. We knew him best when he and Mary lived at Shipley, near us at West Grinstead. He was a very dear friend, not least in the quiet comfort he gave our son when he became seriously ill. He prayed every day for those he knew who needed help, and there were many. He kept a list. He had so many friends and each felt he or she had his special affection. He possessed intense human sympathy, particularly for those who were in difficulties and knew not how to cope. He would go out of his way to sustain them.

Many friends leave their mark in our lives by shared experiences and through mutual affection. Simon gave more than this, for he offered constant love and interest and concern, so that troubles and worries which afflict us all seemed to diminish in his presence. He had the gift of love and peace, of truth and beauty. He left a storehouse of memories upon which we may always draw, and that will last as long as we live.

Bishop of Horsham (2)

PETER ADDENBROOKE

Simon gave as much attention to and could feel as much at home with the more ordinary members of the community, whether church or otherwise, as with the folk at Balmoral. This collection of recollections is from the perspective of one who was not, as the *Telegraph* obituary put it, one of 'the good and the great' to whom Simon was expected particularly to minister during his time, yet to come, in Lincoln. It is rather from the perspective of the Horsham curate who worked at probably the poorest end of the town in what was probably the most community-based of the churches. In some ways that particularly characterized Simon, as I reflect reading again the *Telegraph* obituary.

I met Simon first when I went up to Trinity, Cambridge, in September 1956 as a rather 'green' and young ex-public school boy. I was exempted National Service and so was almost as young as one could be. I believe that in the distribution of undergraduates between himself and the other chaplain, Eric James, I would normally have fallen into his group, having a surname in the first part of the alphabet. However I was assigned to Eric James. This was perhaps because my father was known to be a clergyman of the Church of England, and I had made it clear that I might be of a more questioning type in my membership of the Christian community of the college, perhaps more rebellious against the beliefs than some of the more mainstream upholders of the faith. I joined one of what were called the 'cells' of the college Christian community only on condition that I could question every aspect of the faith which it might have been presumed we all shared. From time to time we would be honoured with a visit from one of the Chaplains; or we might invite Harry Williams to share in our free-ranging discussions of what seemed to us the current issues of the faith: for instance, whether to 'have sex' with the current girlfriend and what might be thought of that by our contemporaries. That now seems thoroughly dated, since it was before the freedom of the 1960s enabled by the 'pill'. Among those whom we invited to join our discussions would have been Simon, though I have no clear memory of that. Those who attended the early communion service in the college chapel would also get invited to breakfast with one of the Chaplains; and in this way I believe I must have met Simon, though I suspect rather shyly.

The first clear memory I carry of Simon is of his return to preach at Great St Mary's, Cambridge, soon after the beginning of his time in Coventry, which must have been in 1959 before I had left Trinity. The text has always stayed with me, and also seems to characterize what Simon was prepared to do. 'And the people stood afar off, and Moses drew near unto the thick darkness where God was' (Exodus 20.21). He used this text to characterize what it was like to enter into an industrial community from which the Church was estranged. His conviction, which was vividly conveyed to the undergraduates

1 Simon's grandmother, Mrs Wilton Phipps, painted by John Singer Sargent

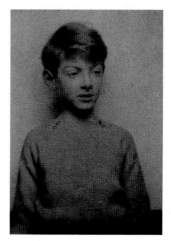

2 Aged 6

3 At Heatherdown Prep School

4 About to leave Eton

5 In Highland dress

6 Lt Simon Phipps, Coldstream Guards

7 With Eric James at Trinity College,
Cambridge

U PHIPPS I

July the Sixth ! S. Phipps is twenty-eight !
— In fancy Westcott, stage for Pulpit spurns :—
Gaitered or gartered, flags and cheers await
His Many Happy Returns.

8 Cartoon

9 Being offered a Stirrup Cup by David Smith of the Wheatsheaf pub, Louth, 1976

10 Chaplain at Trinity College, Cambridge

11 The new Bishop of Lincoln

12 At Simon Phipps's consecration in Lincoln Cathedral

13 Simon and
Mary Phipps
at home at Shipley

14 Christening of Ian
and Caroline Gilmour's
grandchild Jamie, son
of Peter and Jane
Pleydell-Bouverie

15 The Runcies with
Simon and Mary in
the Gilmours' garden

I'm a Botticelli angel and I'm – BORED
At looking sweet, and faintly overawed :
      I feel so BLOODY silly
       Holding up my Eaden lily
In the way that Botticelli
                 So adored

My girl friend (on that cloud there – with a sword)
Got so sleepy at a sitting that she – SNORED :
       And of course that drove old Botti
        Absolutely potty —
He was tir<u>i</u>d, and my dear,
          I simply ROARED

For the angel
himself

16 Botticelli Angel

listening at his feet, was that in the unchurched community, which the industrial world of Coventry represented, God was as much present already and as much to be found as in any other place, church or otherwise, in this world of ours and God's. Simon was always a master at finding a telling metaphor or picture with which to convey his convictions about the faith. So this was evidence of his courage and conviction in taking on a world to which he was previously a stranger. I was impressed.

My next encounter with Simon was following his appointment as Bishop of Horsham in 1968. In the meantime I had reversed my previous conviction that I would not follow in my father's footsteps, had trained at Lichfield and had served my first curacy in Bakewell. Then, seeking a team ministry, I had moved to Horsham. I experienced the appointment of the first Bishop of Horsham in the shape of Simon with a sense of relief that perhaps the Church of England could sometimes make a good and wise decision. It seemed we were to be blessed; and indeed we were. For though I had not read *God on Monday* I was aware that we would have a man who cared for his people and was aware of the problems of presenting the faith to an increasingly unchurched population. Or rather I should be saying that it was for Simon a matter of discovering where the faith lay in these people and in what ways God was already represented and present among them. His capacity for radical theology, his experience of industrial chaplaincy, his capacity to enter into the darkness and the unknown, his sensitivity to the poetic and his ability to create a picture, all of these would be an enormous relief to someone who found himself among some, at times, very prosaic colleagues.

Part of his induction to the suffragan bishopric was to be his enthronement in his chair, his 'cathedra', at St Mary's, Horsham. I found myself assigned (or was it chosen by the bishop as it certainly felt?) to be his chaplain for the service – a completely unfamiliar role for me. He seemed to treat me as a close colleague, someone known and met long ago, now in surroundings familiar to me and new to him. What I remember of my encounter is his telling of choosing his 'purple'.

As a part of his preparation for his new role he had to obtain the right clothes. To this end he went to a clerical outfitters. Here he was shown by a doting assistant the enormous variety of shades of the colour purple which were available for the fabrication of his shirts. Finding the choice bewildering, with a mimed gesture – to me – he threw a swatch of material over his shoulder, drawing it around him and saying to the surprised assistant with a voice and tone which were his most fey, 'But darling; I don't think this is quite me!' The curate had to be told to keep his laughter in the vestry quiet please! 'Footlights' had somehow got into St Mary's vestry. His masterly capacity for acting the part was also displayed in the total and committed seriousness with which he took his part in the service which followed.

Many times has Simon's capacity for pastoral ministry been reported. I can only add my contribution to other reports. Remaining the awkward individual I had always been, asking questions which others didn't like and choosing radical theology in a diocese which was largely traditional and conservative in a number of senses, my choice of looking outside the usual training channels of the Church for pastoral skills and insights was not always welcomed. I found myself not always happy in my curate's lot. It was my wife Mary who encouraged me to seek the counsel of this apparently accessible and understanding bishop we had been blessed with. So I tried him out. I asked to see him and was offered an appointment a few weeks ahead. With some trepidation I approached Bishop's House, Worth, and was welcomed with a reserved warmth by this familiar figure. I was asked to sit down in an armchair with a cup of tea and invited to speak about myself and my situation. I found that, contrary to my expectation and in spite of the 'distance' between bishop and curate, I felt free to speak my mind. Contrary to my conscious expectation I was not told that I had got the wrong end of the stick or that my conflicts with the currently popular expressions of the faith were heretical, but rather encouraged to go on exploring as my personal journey took me. And this hour being ended, I was invited to come again in perhaps about six weeks to see 'how things were going'. I found this both a relief and totally unexpected. And this was a repeated experience. Of course with hindsight we can see that this was the experience of many others.

However, if you should gain the impression from this account that Simon was only interested in the welfare of his clergy you would be misinformed. For having become Bishop of Horsham he also took an interest in the families of his clergy. This was a real and genuine interest conveyed by his visit to our house on the estate where we lived with our two young children, a 'semi'. We invited him for a meal. To our surprise he accepted. When he came he seemed clearly at home both with us the adults, but also with the children who could, if they took a dislike to a visitor, play up in no uncertain terms. They took to Simon and he to them. We took him to our hearts. Others like us were also invited to enjoy his hospitality at gatherings, supper parties for the clergy of his area. He was an excellent cook and served up good nourishment not only from the pulpit but also in a most practical and tasty form from his kitchen. Bishop's House knew much merriment even if people also brought their sadnesses and distresses there too.

He won hearts too with the metaphors he could find. I remember that from time to time he would try out his ideas before he used them. On one occasion he had been asked to take the funeral of an incumbent who had been single and like any of those who live alone become quite individual in his ways. Simon's gift was to find the apt image or metaphor for this man. He wondered if he might refer to him as a true eccentric, amplifying this by saying that 'he was a man who knew where the true centre was'. Thus he chose an image that was accurate mechanically as well as giving a true picture of this very individual of individuals.

Parallel with his practical pastoral ministry, he took an interest in new developments for the mutual support of clergy. Over time I had been 'counselled' by Deryck Hutchinson, a Canon of Chichester Cathedral, and when he died I was invited to join a group of clergy whose leadership he would have shared with Mary Welch, a Jungian analyst as well as an experienced marriage counsellor at the Tavistock Clinic, later of course to marry Simon. This group came to find its task as that of sharing experiences, usually on what is often called a 'case-discussion' basis, of their pastoral work in the parish. This enabled the members to get help with the entanglements and problems which arose in the course of a pastoral ministry where much was expected of them but little given in the form

of training. And this not least because the Church had theological language to proclaim its message and to put across the
beliefs to be held by those seeking baptism, marriage or funeral
in church, but no adequate language for the ordinary emo-
tional entanglements experienced in the complex relationships
developed between a pastor and his people. As this group grew
in strength and importance and attracted to its membership
both the principal and vice-principal of Chichester Theological College, so it also came to the attention of the diocesan
bishop and was made the 'baby' of Simon Phipps. When I
made it clear that I would be interested in helping this work to
grow and develop, I was certainly encouraged by Simon and
supported in this aim by him.

Simon's farewell present to me was to sit with him in his
study at Bishop's House, Worth, during one of the regular
sessions which he invited me to schedule with him every six
weeks or so, and to listen to part of the Concerto for Double
String Orchestra by Michael Tippett – I think the final movement. There is a theme which occurs and recurs which seems
to point to hope following sadness – entirely appropriate to the
occasion.

I had no knowledge at that time that Simon and Mary
would return and live for many years in retirement just down
the road from us at Sarsens in Shipley, and that we should in
the future have many happy times together, meeting them
both there, in our own home and when on holiday in France at
Menerbes in Provence. (Though reading this through, I am
reminded that Mary's response to my distress at their leaving
was that there would be time enough – in which she was, and
wasn't, right.) That time was for us a sad loss, even if it was

Lincoln's gain. We did get invited to the installation, being given what seemed places of honour among the many honoured guests. Maybe that was Simon's gift, a gift he also shared with Mary. Everyone he met he made to feel special.

To recollect and write of Simon's time in Horsham could not be complete for me without mention of the retirement years of which there were many. For during Mary's and his own latter years we had many opportunities to meet them, to go to parties given by them on a variety of occasions, to invite them to our house and to find ourselves referred to as 'family'. There were, as Mary had predicted, many hours to share much together and to enjoy their company and friendship when work no longer pressed in the way it had before. The formal relationship engendered between a bishop and his clergy and their families ended with their retirement, but still there remained the warmth and humour, friendliness and affection to be enjoyed – even if it did seem that Simon was too young to leave us when he did.

Bishop of Lincoln (1)

DAVID TUSTIN

After several years as suffragan Bishop of Horsham in the Chichester diocese, Simon was translated to Lincoln and spent twelve years (1974–86) overseeing the largest diocese of the Church of England – largest that is by area rather than population. It may have seemed odd that someone whose earlier ministry had been rooted in the urban and industrial scene should be appointed to such a rural diocese. However, it should be remembered that half the population of Lincoln diocese was (and still is) urban or suburban, and that for many years Scunthorpe had been at the forefront of industrial mission. Simon's appointment made more sense than might at first sight appear. In fact he found great happiness and fulfilment there. Let me try to sketch in some of the light and shade of his ministry in those Lincoln years.

Simon's style was epitomized by the cope and mitre he wore on nearly every occasion – what some irreverently called his 'lemon meringue'! Its colour (pale daffodil, without any embroidery) was *understated*, whilst its design was *bravely contemporary*. That was Simon to a tee! His half-sized shepherd's crook gave a hint of his reluctance to play up to the strong lead many people expected. The leadership he gave was of a quite different kind. Beneath his easy and unassuming appearance lay a warm-hearted and sensitive person, simple yet profound, visionary and full of insight – a gracious and courteous radical. His agenda was God-centred and world-centred, rather than Church-centred.

At heart he was an unusually humble person, thoroughly realistic in his estimate of what he could and could not do. In his first years at Lincoln he worked out what kind of diocesan bishop he had it in him to be, and then concentrated on making that distinctive contribution. He went to as few meetings of diocesan committees as he decently could. Some were unavoidable, and under his chairmanship the Bishop's Council often went round and round in a morass of ever-recurring issues. He knew this was not his forte, and regarded himself (in his own words) as an 'administrative muddler'. Nevertheless, he certainly had his own vision of where the diocese should go, and gained many people's confidence by his warmth and openness, and by the trust he placed in them. Several of his initiatives left their mark, especially in the key areas of ministry, ecumenism, education and pastoral care.

Simon was the first bishop in England to set up a major local ministry scheme. Southwark diocese had earlier run a pilot project involving just four worker-priests, and Norwich was experimenting with rural groups. In the early 1980s Lincoln diocese embarked on a much broader scheme combining both local ordained and local lay ministers, with the Revd Laurie Blanchard as its director. This far-reaching development led the field nationally.

Simon was also a keen advocate of women's ministry. As early as 1978 he licensed Miss Peggy Hartley at Bracebridge

Heath as the first woman 'minister-in-charge' of a parish. Before ordination services at Lincoln Cathedral he often used to take part in the outdoor prayer vigil organized by the Movement for the Ordination of Women. He paved the way for women priests to become eventually well accepted in the diocese, where most churchmanship was broadly Catholic.

Equally positive was Simon's contribution to Christian unity. He played a vital role in bringing to life the sponsoring body for ecumenical projects – one of the first in the country. He succeeded in winning the friendship and confidence of other denominational leaders, and with them entered a public covenant to act jointly wherever possible. He took the bold step of appointing a United Reformed minister, the Revd Richard Taylor, as St Hugh's Missioner and canon of the cathedral. At the suggestion of Canon John Nurser he also embarked on the three-way link with the Roman Catholic diocese of Brugge in West Flanders and that of Nottingham. Simon found a kindred spirit in his Belgian counterpart, Mgr de Smedt, who had been one of the progressive voices at the Second Vatican Council. This partnership bore fruit at many levels.

Another major emphasis of Simon's episcopate was adult education. To him the resourcing of lay Christians for their daily witness in the world was paramount. He keenly promoted the Bishop's Certificate course and a series of training days for churchwardens, which were widely taken up. With this went his restructuring of the education team, which had been in some disarray. He also encouraged the Regional House under the Revd (now Canon) Stephen Phillips at Great Limber, and was personally involved in many consultations organized by Canon Rex Davis at Edward King House, Lincoln, on contemporary issues. At all levels he treated people as responsible adults, capable of thinking for themselves and shouldering greater responsibility.

Two important developments were begun with the help of his wife Mary, who was a psychotherapist. One was the establishment of a network for pastoral care and counselling, which made skilled counselling readily available to clergy and their families. The other was to start a system for clergy to appraise their own ministry with the help of trained advisers. Although both projects lacked the firmer shape which his successor Bishop Robert Hardy rightly gave them, to Simon must go the credit for discerning the way forward, and for having the courage to take these new initiatives when such developments were not yet widespread.

Simon is well remembered in the diocese for his warm personal links with the parishes, especially with clergy and their families. His custom was to block off one or two complete days every month for the sole purpose of visiting clergy in their own homes. Even though he had never run an ordinary parish, he was an experienced and insightful pastor. In a relaxed and natural way his loving kindliness communicated across the usual boundaries, and included the children of clergy families. People could sense that he carried them in his prayers, which he certainly did with great discipline and devotion, after the pattern of his beloved predecessor, Bishop Edward King. Because of an innate trust in the basic goodness of human nature Simon was generous to a fault. He gave a second chance to many clergy who had experienced difficulties, and in cases requiring discipline was inclined to be too soft. It was characteristic of him that he spent his sabbatical as a hospital chaplain in Edinburgh, working under expert supervision, sharpening his own pastoral skills.

Simon was strong on vision, weak on practicalities. His senior suffragan, Gerald Colin (Bishop of Grimsby 1965–78), is said to have remarked more than once at staff meetings, 'Simon, you're flying at 5,000 feet. Come down to earth!' In fact, Simon had a real skill in holding together a team of very diverse colleagues, and in creating the atmosphere within which disagreements could be frankly shared and ideas sharpened into practical application. He tended to consult and consult, but took ages to decide. He was generous in the time he spent 'one-to-one' with his archdeacons, suffragans and principal officers. He made sure that each of them knew not only what they were doing, but also what *he* felt about it. In large measure he trusted them to get on in their own way, but not without showing continuing interest.

There can be no doubt that Simon was enormously enriched by his partnership with Mary. They had married only a short while before coming to Lincoln, when he had turned 50 and she had already turned 60. Theirs was a mature and fiercely loyal relationship, in which ideas were tossed around in a sparky way. Each was their own person, and in reinforcing one another they were a powerful mix. Some clergy seemed terrified that Mary would psychoanalyse them if they so much as opened their mouths. In fact, she and Simon observed very strict professional boundaries, and many individuals in deep need were greatly helped by her skill as a psychotherapist. During their Lincoln years, rather than taking a weekly day off, they used to spend a block of several days every month at

Shipley in Sussex – resting, reading, thinking, writing – recharging their batteries. They greatly loved that spot, and eventually retired there.

One of the high points of Simon and Mary's unique and accomplished style of hospitality was the ordination retreat. Since they had no children, the ordinands and their wives were able to stay in Bishop's House itself. It was more like a house party than a traditional retreat. Whilst serious in intent, these were joyous occasions with a good deal of hilarity – a great bonding experience for those who took part. Simon and Mary's public farewell in the cathedral nave took an unusual but very appropriate form: it was not a eucharist but an informal 'agape' meal – like a rather classy musical picnic, gathered deanery by deanery. This happy and memorable occasion well symbolized Simon and Mary's joint approach.

Simon's rapport with the people of Lincolnshire and South Humberside as a whole was a matter on which opinions varied widely. There was no question that he could relate with ease and naturalness alike to the aristocracy or to the working people of farm or factory. However, he chose not to socialize with the gentry in quite the way his predecessor had done, and this caused some disappointment. In view of his patrician background, people perhaps expected him to be more 'establishment' than he was. It was not a simple question of political differences, but rather of his not fitting the usual categories known to Lincolnshire. He came across so differently to different people. If some found it hard to understand 'where he was coming from', this failure of appreciation may well have been to some extent mutual. Whatever the explanation, one thing is certain: he really loved the villages and market towns of his diocese every bit as much as the urban or industrial scene. He relished spending much of his time out and about, meeting people, and was concerned for the diocese as a whole, not just Lincoln as its centre. He took a real delight in motoring to remote country churches, and came to enjoy the particular beauties of the Lincolnshire heath, wold, marsh and fen.

Two basic convictions underlay Simon's whole ministry. Because he believed that Christ died not for the Church but for the world, he was passionately convinced that the Church must take the initiative to engage with the world, and never rest content within its own circle. He tried to touch parts of society that the Church does not usually touch. This was the motive for his liberal openness, his willingness to embrace and his inclusive care for ordinary people. Secondly, he tried – like the first apostles – to stand for the resurrection. He saw it as his main task to bring hope, affirmation, encouragement and reassurance to people in a wide range of situations.

It is sad that Simon's qualities were not universally appreciated, indeed were sometimes misunderstood. In some ways his effectiveness was limited. Yet many people in the Lincoln diocese treasure very positive memories about him: his graciousness and openness; his imagination and courage; his lightness of touch and gently self-mocking humour; the immense trouble he took to understand, to help and to reassure. He was a modest and godly man, true to the gifts God gave him. He dedicated himself utterly to trying to be – in his own distinctive way – all that a bishop should be, without clinging to the prestige of that office.

It was very fitting that his last visit to Lincoln was to take part in the eighth centenary of St Hugh's death in November

2000. He seemed content as he reflected back over the good work that he and Mary together had done there. Her death the previous June had been a shattering blow for him, and he was ready to depart in peace.

Bishop of Lincoln (2)

ALAN DUTFIELD

During the whole of my full-time ministry I have been haunted by a feeling that I am not really a proper clergyman, unlike that young fellow with his black suit, detailed knowledge of the correct wear for all occasions, sacred and profane, and of much more trivia. I have found moreover, by careful soundings, that I am not entirely alone in this feeling. My knowledge of Simon is that of one of his parish priests whom he treated (as he did so many) as a friend, and I had an increasing feeling that he was one of us; in his case feeling that he was not really a proper bishop! I've no doubt that in him the feeling was based on a real humility.

This may well account for his acceptance of 'bullying' by his staff. That this happened was widely believed, and confirmed after Simon phoned me one day to suggest that I had a look at a student from the theological college with a view to taking him as curate. I phoned the college and, since the man was free the following day, fetched him and put him through our parochial selection process. The verdict was 'tough but we can cope', and we agreed there and then that he should join us. The following morning Simon rang me to say that he had been 'jumped on' by his staff, who did not want this man in the diocese. He did not seem unduly distressed when I pointed out that he was too late, and that we could not be expected to go back on our arrangement. Eventually the young man was appointed to a senior living in the diocese!

It may have been to this episode that one of the staff members referred when he told me that the staff had had a bad couple of days, for they had to leave Simon on his own, and he had created chaos in their absence. It is worth noting that later, when he instituted a scheme under which the staff went together on an annual retreat, and were paired to act as fathers in God to each other, Simon was paired with this particular member, who became as a result devoted to his bishop.

On another occasion I arrived early at church for the 10 a.m. service one Sunday, to find Mary and Simon alighting from their car. I expressed my pleasure at seeing them, but asked why they were there. He said, 'Aren't I doing a confirmation?' I assured them that he wasn't, and so they decided to join the congregation. (It afterwards transpired that he'd pencilled the date in his diary, changed it, and forgotten to erase the entry.) What followed was entirely pleasurable, and after the service they and the congregation enjoyed one another over coffee. Before leaving, Simon expressed his and Mary's delight at an unexpected pleasure, and I remarked that this seemed to be a very proper and useful activity for a bishop, and wouldn't it be good to set aside a few Sundays each year for such visits? He thought not, and I sympathized with the problems of a packed diary. He replied that the diary wasn't the problem. 'They'd think I was spying.' I think he sadly underestimated the power of his humble loving humanity.

When Simon was appointed to Lincoln I, like many others,

wondered what on earth we had got! Our ideas were con-
ditioned by what we had read not long before about his relationship with Princess Margaret, and we were suspicious.
My ideas were crystallized and corrected by an episode at a
Swanwick diocesan conference. This had been arranged for a
few months after our new bishop's advent, giving him (sparse)
time to visit all the clergy first. This he had done, giving on
average some 30 minutes to an hour to each of the 200 or so
we then had. At lunchtime my routine attempt to arrange my
queuing to avoid sitting with 'top brass' failed spectacularly,
for I found myself sitting next to Mary and directly opposite
Simon. I started the conversation by saying that I'd been
impressed by her husband's memory, adding that 'I wouldn't
be surprised to find that he knows the names of very many of
the clergy here.' Mary suggested that we ask him, and did so.
Simon thought for a moment, and replied, 'I know the names
of all the clergy; I'm not sure about a few of the lay people' (of
whom there were about a hundred).

I realised by then that when he knew the names it meant
that he also knew the names of their wives and their families,
and much of their circumstances. I suggested to Mary that this
was a remarkable gift. She replied, 'No, no, he does it by
praying for them.' And I knew then much more about the sort
of bishop we had.

8 The Friend

Marriage

STEPHEN VERNEY

I can say with many others that Simon was one of my best friends. But I had a unique privilege: that he came and talked over with me the most important step in his life. Should he or should he not risk taking the plunge into marriage? And when he and Mary had decided to marry he asked me to be his best man.

We met first at Westcott House, where we arrived together as 'new boys', feeling shy, and knowing nothing of theology. He helped me to laugh and to see the funny side of reading theology, to take oneself less seriously as we got deeper into the mystery of Jesus. I remember a seminar where four of us were studying St John with Harry Williams, and we all, Harry and the rest of us, broke down in helpless laughter round Simon's comments. Perhaps we got deeper into the mystery that day.

After we left Westcott we kept in touch, and one August Simon came and led an international youth camp in my parish. It rained for most of the month that Simon was with us, and he camped in the mud with some 20 young people from different countries and churches and helped them to build our new church on a Nottingham housing estate. Under Simon's leadership the whole event became a vision of the

Kingdom of God, with the reality of good breaking down barriers and overcoming the reality of evil. I remember one of the girls saying, in her broken English, 'The Church in my country is very bad', and how by the end of the month we had come to experience, across all the barriers, our oneness and our amazing happiness in the real Church.

But to return to his marriage. Simon was very attractive to girls, and he had many friends who were girls, one of whom, as everybody knew, was Princess Margaret. But in his relations with them was a certain shyness – or was it a certain respect based on his humility about himself, and arising out of his humour which did not take himself too seriously? He did not believe that he could really be worth loving. In Mary I guess that he met somebody who with all her psychological understanding saw into the depths where he had never before allowed anyone to enter, and who loved the real Simon behind his humour and his humility.

So began a marriage which was a love affair. Mary needed Simon as much as he needed her. But like all real love it was difficult, and after a couple of months Simon was in despair. Had they made an enormous mistake? Then gradually these two remarkable and original people adjusted to each other, and there followed years of creative partnership and ever-deepening happiness. When Mary died Simon was bereft, and he did not long survive her.

The Family Friend

DAVID GILMOUR

Simon Phipps christened me, married me and christened my two eldest children. I have always been proud of this record and must have boasted of the first of these ceremonies at an early age. Simon once recalled how my younger brother Oliver ran tearfully to our mother for reassurance: 'Mr Pips did born me, Mummy, didn't he?' But the privilege had been mine alone. Oliver had not been 'borned' by Mr Pips.

As children we were hardly aware that Simon was a clergyman. We never saw him in a dog-collar or behaving like a vicar in church. My father began calling him 'Bishop' at least a decade before he was appointed to such an office because he thought he deserved the title. But that seemed to us the only clerical thing about him.

Simon was a gentle and delightful friend for small children. He joined in games, he told funny stories, he clowned in front of the cameras, making faces or wearing a tweed cap the wrong way round. Headgear was an important part of his costume: he often wore a beret or a straw hat, which he sometimes swam in.

Once or twice, in my grandparents' house in Scotland, we were allowed to stay up after dinner to watch Simon perform his 'tricks', sketches from his Cambridge days in the

Footlights. I still remember some of them 40 years later: the startled pheasant, the general reviewing his troops, the old woman with her shopping bags in a telephone box talking on and on while an impatient queue lines up outside. We thought him hilarious – the funniest man we knew. His enactment of scenes from *Monsieur Hulot's Holiday* was much funnier than the film itself.

His humour, while essentially adult, was easily adapted to please children. As a small boy I was surprised when he once insisted on shaking hands with me. It was the inauguration of a private joke that outlasted my childhood. Bending his middle finger into the palm of his hand, he shook mine with the words, ' 'Scuse the wart.' I guffawed and soon began playing the trick on my schoolfellows.

When I was about 10 we saw a different side of Simon. In 1963 he had told the Coventry North Conservative Association that he was going to vote Labour at the next general election. Shortly afterwards he came to stay with us in Norfolk and, while he was driving Oliver and me to a service in Norwich Cathedral, I am alleged to have turned to my brother and said, 'Do you realize we have a red-hot socialist in the car?' I do not remember this myself, but I expect it was true: I was naturally a Conservative at the time because my father had just won a by-election for the Tories in Central Norfolk.

In the same period we were taken to see Simon at work, when he was Industrial Chaplain at Coventry. He showed us round the new cathedral, and I recall being overawed by the great Graham Sutherland tapestry behind the altar. But as I nearly always saw him in the school holidays, I remember him in his leisure much more clearly than in his work.

During the late 1960s my family spent Augusts in a house on the northeast coast of Majorca. The 'Bishop', who usually visited us there, quickly became '*el Obispo*' and once had his ring kissed by a devout boatman. (I think by that time he must have become a suffragan bishop.) But my other memories of Simon in Spanish waters are secular – of clowning on picnics in his beret or his straw hat, of his brave but inelegant and unskilful water-skiing, of getting badly sunburnt – 'Cover the Bishop's angry feet' was a familiar cry after they had been exposed for a day or two in the sun.

It would be misleading to write that Simon mellowed in middle age, because that would suggest he had been unmellow before. The truth is that he became even mellower, just as he became even gentler, as he got older. His humour, like his charm and his infectious laugh, remained, but he made fewer funny faces and – a great blow this – he no longer performed his 'tricks'. A representative image of Simon in about 1980 would show him at an easel, slightly stooped and wearing a panama hat, painting an olive grove in Tuscany or Provence.

As I grew older, I realized that, on secular matters at least, he resembled Landor: 'Nature I loved, and, next to Nature, Art.' He loved paintings and looked at them wisely, concentrating on one or two in a room and finding things in them that had eluded less patient inspectors. He loved music too and, although he was entirely untaught, he played the piano by ear with great verve.

I remember Simon often gazing at views, which his wife Mary encouraged him to paint in middle age. Moved by natural beauty, he was inevitably saddened by the desecration of the countryside. Once we were at Boughton in Northamptonshire, standing at the centre of a wood from which the radiating rides had been planned in straight lines, each ending with a distant view of a church tower. But now two of the rides ended with vistas of factories, and two more had no view at all. Simon looked with melancholy at the scene and murmured, 'And they call it progress.'

Mary came into his life at about the same time that my wife Sarah came into mine. She and Simon were a gentle and harmonious presence, wise and tolerant and appreciative of beautiful places. They embodied a wisdom and a serenity that, however unattainable to most of us, one felt one should at least strive for. They were able to enjoy the leisure of old age because they learned the secret of how to grow old together.

Holidays in France

JOE DOWNING

No one could have been more English than Simon and Mary Phipps, but it would be hard to find a couple who so much loved France and things French, and it was in France, in Menerbes, when both were visiting Peter and Rosemary Montagnon, that they decided to continue their lives together. It was at this time that we met, and my friend Emmanuel and I looked forward each year to their returning to Menerbes with the same pleasure that we awaited spring, and not only because they came bearing chocolates for Emmanuel and Bath Olivers for me. We loved them both. I would cook for them and Mary would cook for us, and we would drink totally unreasonable quantities of the Maubert white wine from Goult that we were all so fond of.

Simon's pencil drawings were of professional quality and he was a very good amateur painter. He would go off in the mornings, wearing an old straw hat and sandals with some cool old clothing in between, bearing his painting gear and glowing with happy anticipation, for several hours of landscape work, forgetting everything as he often told me except the joys and the problems of rendering and translating what he saw and felt. Mary would be waiting with a good summer lunch.

She encouraged him in his painting and was proud of the results.

In later years Simon and Mary gave us the pleasure of coming twice a year, each trip carefully and voluptuously prepared in every detail: where to stop off on the way, where one might best eat and sleep, the sites of the great cathedrals. For the return voyages Emmanuel would be of help, and their pleasure in the planning was a foretaste of that of being in the places chosen.

When Simon knew he was going to retire he said to us, 'You must come for a weekend to Lincoln while I still have the keys to everything.' So we did, and it was unforgettable. Mary's cooking, delicious and more subdued under British skies; the great moving beauty of the cathedral; being served breakfast in bed on a Sunday morning by a bishop on his way to work.

Conjugal complicity is moving, admirable to see, and Simon and Mary possessed the quality bountifully. As they aged, Simon was discreetly protective of Mary's frailty and, as were we all, proud of her strength; her serene gaze never faltered, nor did her warm dignity.

In speaking of Mary I speak of Simon, for I knew them only together. Mary had been hesitant about their marriage. She still mourned James whom she had loved; but she found another love for Simon, and they were a delight to see together, each a protector and a shield, and caring deeply for each other. When I learned that Simon had died so soon after Mary's decease I was not surprised. Their mutual need had become absolute, and they were gone on the only trip whose least detail they had not been able to plan.

Home at Shipley

MORFA POPE

We came to Shipley where Dan my husband was vicar in 1992 via 20 years in Radley, Oxfordshire, and a brief time in northern Cyprus, and in Shipley we had the happiest eight years. It is a unique and beautiful parish. Simon and Mary had lived there for many years; they were part of the magic.

We met Simon on our first day on a parish walk. 'Call me Simon', he said – a gesture typical of his openness and modesty; and we three walked together for some time and began a deep and wonderful friendship with both Simon and Mary. Within days we were invited to a delicious summer supper with asparagus and strawberries picked locally early that morning by Mary, already in her eighties. We certainly touched the enchanted cord and shared many mutual interests in the arts, and, particularly, a deep appreciation of the Welsh poet and priest, R.S. Thomas. His poetry was subsequently read at Dan's funeral and at both Mary's and Simon's.

Simon was much loved and appreciated in Shipley parish where he gave his help unstintingly. He was deeply caring, sensitive and thoughtful, also very witty, funny and human. He was forward-thinking in his theology and very much in line with the (now) newly appointed Archbishop of

Canterbury, Dr Rowan Williams. He had a great sense of occasion in church, and to see Simon and Dan together at major festivals, particularly in their richly coloured robes, was a most beautiful spectacle. On one of those occasions Mary whispered to me, 'Isn't it good that they are both such great friends.'

On our golden wedding anniversary they gave us an amazing lunch to which they asked over 20 of our close friends. Simon made eight huge summer puddings, and during a speech said, 'We loved doing this but I hope we shall never have to do it again.' They had taken a week to make the preparations for this memorable meal. We gave Simon and Mary a party on their silver wedding anniversary starting with a drinks party for about 25 people and followed by a dinner party for six of their special friends. We were delighted to do this, and I think they much enjoyed the whole occasion.

Mary was ten years older than Simon and she was already very tired and frail, but when she died in the summer of 2000 Simon was devastated and so, so lonely. He spent a great deal of time with us, and did marathon work in the parish as Dan's health was failing (he died in November 2000). Simon and our bishop, Lindsay Urwin, took the funeral most beautifully, and yet again Simon was in charge of the parish. He always saw the need and as Dan used to say 'was prepared to run the second mile'.

He died, quite unexpectedly in January 2001, waiting for a dear friend for supper with everything prepared. He was found in his armchair in the library. It was a terrible shock for her, and the most dreadful loss for us all. He was a great man, a true servant of God and deeply loved and appreciated by all who knew him.

Simon and Mary will always be deeply missed in the parish of Shipley to which they gave so much. We all loved them.

Epilogue: Sermons and Prayers

Sermon Preached at Mary Welch's (Phipps) Funeral, 20 June 2000

DAVID WILCOX

> To discover how to be human now is the reason we follow this star.
>
> (W.H. Auden)

> Underneath are the everlasting arms.
>
> (Deuteronomy 33.27)

What memories we all have of this shy, kind friendly person! And what an extraordinary and varied life was hers! I shall try, as best I can, to pick out some of the episodes from Mary's life which were, I believe, highly significant and formative. (There are big gaps in this account, e.g. France, which she dearly loved.)

The first episode occurred when she was a child, about eight years old. Mary was going to church with her grandmother, in Oxfordshire, one Sunday evening in summer. Her Granma left her briefly to take some food to a woman who was ill. The church bells were ringing for the evening service. Quite suddenly it dawned upon Mary: 'My Granma will die!' This childhood experience brought an awareness of death, and I think it is true to say that thereafter Mary thought about death almost daily. It was also an experience of being outside time: the facts of her own birth and of her own death were present in that present moment. It was a spiritual experience, but a frightening and lonely one. Mary told me that it marked a kind of BC/AD in her life and that the accompanying feeling, 'I can't manage this at all', went on for years afterwards. But underneath were the everlasting arms.

The next episode is a happier one and helped her, I think, to begin to come to terms with her fear and her inner loneliness. Mary went to boarding school at Moira House in Eastbourne. There, her peers were in the practice of going to church, but Mary did not want to go to church. The headmistress, a wise and good person, agreed that, instead, she should read a book on her own for an hour and then talk with her about it. One of those books, if you will believe me, was Aldous Huxley's *Perennial Philosophy* – being read by a child of 12!

But the point is that what Mary encountered here at Moira House was human understanding. And in that headmistress a motherly figure, who welcomed her, understood her, was interested in her. Someone understood.

She went on to RADA and then on to the West End stage. Her first marriage was to Godfrey Tearle, the actor, and producer of Shakespeare plays at the Royal Court Theatre. She also played a lot of Shakespeare in Regent's Park. I suppose that her deep knowledge and love of Shakespeare and of poetry dates from schooldays, but it must have been enormously enhanced in those acting years. Mary told me: 'If I don't read poetry, I feel I have betrayed something.' She continued to read verse throughout her life: Shelley, Keats, R.S. Thomas, W.H. Auden. Until fairly recently, she would still read poetry

aloud most beautifully during Quiet Days led by Simon. In
supervisions too – just leaving a line from a poem hanging
there. I think she responded especially to R.S. Thomas, with
his bleak and questioning belief, testing her own faith on
emptiness, 'nailing her questions one by one to an untenanted
cross'. She certainly identified with Auden's three wise men:
'To discover how to be human now is the reason we follow this
star.'

Just after the war, Mary was to be found in a totally different setting – working in the hospital of Holloway prison,
where she was supposed to be nursing. She got sacked within
a week for not getting through her work. And why? Because
she was talking to the patients more than nurses should, or
could. But here was another wise and discerning person. The
matron who sacked her as a nurse invited her to come back
the following week in a different capacity. She gave to Mary a
list of some of the prisoners who should come and talk. And
they came – women who had been allowed out just for one
day to have their babies and then come back, women who
had had abortions, or made suicide attempts. And so began,
without any training and very ad hoc, what was to become
Mary's life work – simply because she was interested in them
and they needed someone to talk to. How often in after
years, how very often, would people say: 'I'd like to talk to
Mary.'

By this time she was married to James Welch, an anthro-
pologist, a priest, who had been Head of Religious Broadcast-
ing, BBC. The Labour government had just started up in East
Africa the ill-fated groundnut scheme. James and Mary went
out to Tanzania and lived for the first two years under canvas,

with water rationed to three gallons a day. The ground was parched and dusty. An African labour force arrived, straight from the bush, some still armed with spears. But there also arrived bewildered English families, wondering where was the nearest shop or school or hairdresser. Morale plummeted, and it was then Mary started really to become aware of people struggling with depression: heavy drinking, broken marriages, rows. She remembers saying to James one day: 'If I ever get out of this alive, I'm going to get some proper training.' The rest, as they say, is history, and many of you here know the story at first-hand because you have shared it with her.

Time does not allow me to tell of her struggling as a psychiatric social worker at St Thomas's hospital, where she firmly rejected William Sargent and his practice of leucotomy (showing the determined, tough, even stubborn side of her character), and eventually of her starting to have her own analysis, her eight years' training and her long association as a training analyst with the Society of Analytical Psychology. (She told the story herself in an interview for its journal, with Marcus West.) Of the early days of training, she says: 'It was like being back at the university I'd never been to. It was marvellous. I loved it.'

The day came when James Welch died, of a heart attack in London, where Mary had a practice. She came down, bereaved, to their home here in Shipley, and found it very difficult to cope with all the well-intentioned letters and reactions she received. Some people got it right. Bob Hobson for one. Camilla Bosanquet rang up. 'I'm at Coolham crossroads', she said, 'I've got a chicken.' Later, they picked crocuses, and the crocuses became wide open – there was life after death. That little story makes me very wary of what I am going to say.

I can almost hear Mary getting ready to break in with 'senti-mental tosh' at any moment.

I have her photograph in front of me – the fine white hair, the beautiful rather gaunt face, her eyes gazing steadily at us, her mouth about to break into a gentle smile, the narrow shoulders. She must have been a very striking woman in her youth. I think she was capable of dazzling. But she knew it, and had for example chosen Fred Plaut as her supervisor because he would be tough with her and be proof against her charm!

Later on, she charmed the bishops, and one in particular! Support groups for the clergy were being set up in the diocese of Southwark and the diocese of Chichester. Mary was, with others, leading the support group for the clergy in the Chichester diocese. Simon was Bishop of Horsham at the time. He told her that after six months he would phone her to see how it was going. After six months exactly, he did just that. They had dinner together, and the personal relationship grew ever closer and warmer.

Many of us here know how astonishing it is to find someone we can love so much, and how much more astonishing it is to find oneself married to someone who loves us so much. So it was, and so it has been for 27 years for Simon and Mary.

She was, I think, a very brave person. We have seen that she could be very frightened. But she used her fears extraordinarily well. Here, latterly, was this rather frail person, like a small bird, and yet tough with an extraordinary powerful spirit. Think of how she recovered from that very serious fracture in France last year. I think her deafness was a great pain and trial to her. But she could stand physical pain and make nothing of it.

One of the things that fascinated Mary was a person's underlying ethos – the question: *what do they live by?* She thought that that was the analyst's particular concern. The analyst asks: 'What makes this person live this particular "myth", this view of life?'

Is it possible to say what was the world-view (the life-truth) that Mary lived by? Human understanding – that's what she really cared about most. 'To discover how to be human now is the reason we follow this star.' People would come to her in a muddle. 'I believe in muddle', she would say. And so she and the client would sit and talk, and Mary would listen. She believed in taking time, keeping things in play, enduring the not-knowing. To help people find their own way: that was her professional practice.

But what she listened out for was the one word or sentence that just encapsulated a lot of other things that they were talking about. There was one occasion (Mary has told this before) when a woman was going through a catalogue of all the things that had gone wrong in her life. 'But what do you feel your life is like now?' The woman said, quite suddenly and angrily: 'Dreggy. That's it, dreggy.' But from that moment in the interview, things seemed to begin to come together, making a sort of pattern out of the dregs, out of the tea leaves. At the end of the interview, the woman was certainly more human, and said Mary, 'I think I was too.'

'Human love', Mary said to me, 'human love – I'd bet my bottom dollar on that.' She told a story about it. There was a soldier serving abroad during the last war, who was writing a letter home. He himself had very little schooling and his wife in Leeds was near-illiterate. This is how he began his letter:

'Dear Lil, I am writing this slow, because I know you read slow.' The man's imagination reached out to his wife in Leeds: 'the holiness of the heart's affection'. Human love. Mary knew only too well that such love could at times be costly, demanding, precarious. It might take you to Africa, into prison, or into the deep dark recesses of another person's anguish. It might also bring you the unspeakable joy of loving and being loved.

The Christian faith bids us believe that such human love, vulnerable, costly and joyful, is a reflection (sometimes a very pale reflection) of a greater love, the love of God himself. Christian faith assures us, indeed, that God *is* Love, that he created this amazing world out of love, and that he once showed us that love most clearly on a cross.

> Here is God; no monarch he
> Throned in easy state to reign.
> Here is God; whose arms of love
> Aching, spent, the world sustain.
>
> (W.H. Vanstone)[1]

Friends, if that is true (and I'd bet my bottom dollar on it) then our loved ones are in even more loving hands than ours. They *and* we are in more loving hands than we have ever known; than we can ever imagine: 'Underneath are the everlasting arms.'

Meanwhile, to discover how to be human now is the reason we follow the star.

---

1 From 'Love's Endeavour, Love's Expense', W.H. Vanstone, 'Hymn 496' in *Hymns Ancient and Modern New Standard* (Norwich: Canterbury Press, 1983).

Sermon Preached at Simon Phipps's Funeral, 12 February 2001

DAVID WILCOX

> I have used the word 'attention' . . . to express the idea of
> a just and loving gaze directed upon an individual reality.
>
> (Iris Murdoch)[1]

My friends, we have come to mourn the sudden loss of a dear friend but also to celebrate a remarkable life. The writer in *The Times* last week struck precisely the right note when he said that Simon combined gentleness, tranquillity and sweetness of character with deep psychological insight and considerable strength of purpose. And, I would add, a deep humility.

As I reflected upon what I know of that life of nearly 80 years, it seems to me that the one word which comes nearest to capturing its meaning is the word 'attention': 'a just and loving gaze directed upon an individual reality'. In the short time we have this afternoon, let's look together at a few episodes in Simon's life.

See him, first of all, just after the war, president of the

---

1 *The Sovereignty of Good* (London: Routledge & Kegan Paul, 1970), p. 34.

Cambridge Footlights, which prepared the way for 'That Was the Week that Was'. See him dressed (or partly dressed) as an artist's model and singing: 'I'm a Botticelli angel and I'm bored . . .' He was, of course, a brilliant mimic. See him, for instance, mimicking Charles Raven, the Regius Professor; sweeping back his gown and telling of some 'profoundly moving occasion' (which happened to Raven rather often). Now, you can't mimic people unless, like Alan Bennett or Simon Phipps, you pay attention to people, to life, to detail.

Returning to Cambridge, after his curacy in Huddersfield, Simon became chaplain in his own college, Trinity, where this capacity for attention, attention to the individual, was very evident, as he concentrated entirely on the person he was speaking to.

The fine obituary to which I referred clearly saw Simon's next work as the happiest of his ministry. I mean his ten years in Coventry as industrial chaplain. He was a member of a very remarkable team of men under Bishop Cuthbert Bardsley, including Provost Williams, Stephen Verney and Edward Patey. It was during this time that Simon wrote his book *God on Monday*. It was here, among the working people of Coventry, that he developed a theology which, to a great extent, remained with him for the rest of his life. It was a theology which saw the priority not as attending to things to do with the Church but rather attending to the Kingdom of God; that is to say, attending to ordinary secular affairs and circumstances and trying to perceive what God is saying in and through them. This gave him an immediate link with ordinary working people, as he sought to address these matters in common or garden language. 'Love', he would say, 'means taking *everybody's* interests seriously.' In these ways, Simon was already giving attention to what lay outside himself, especially people in need. It was a form of love: a just and loving gaze directed upon an individual reality.

In 1968 he came to this part of the country, becoming Bishop of Horsham. It was during this time that Simon saw the vital importance of support groups for the clergy. It was this initiative, in particular, which led to his meeting and eventually falling in love with Mary Welch. At the same time, Simon came to see that there is a proper sense in which a priest, a bishop, needs to pay attention to himself, to himself in his relationships, and this became possible for him very largely through the insights of psychotherapy. Simon wrote:

> Religion *can* become a matter of satisfying a critical God, by adopting a pattern of strict and punishing self-discipline. Then it becomes all rules and regulations which must be obeyed. But what are we playing at out there, when all the time there is God waiting for us in our rejected inner life, where he accepts all the very things that make us afraid?
>
> To be responsible for myself is to face myself and then to go on from there. This can make us more free *from* the illusions of anxiety and thereby more free *for* faith.

In 1973 Simon and Mary entered upon a marriage which lasted for 27 years, ended only by Mary's death last June. It brought to them both, and to many of us, very great happiness, but not without its struggles. Neither Simon nor Mary made any secret of the fact that the early years of their marriage were fraught with difficulties. They came through to a relationship (combining both a closeness and a separateness) which was able to embrace so many of us lovingly, a marriage in which others felt comfortable and loved.

The attention which Simon devoted to Mary in those first years undoubtedly affected the character of his next major ministry, as Bishop of Lincoln from 1974 onwards. He tended in later years to be self-deprecating about his effectiveness as a diocesan bishop, but others would regard such self-criticism as very unfair. During those years, he was responsible for some remarkable initiatives: he pioneered the development of Local Ordained Ministry for that large rural diocese (indeed, it is difficult to see now how it could otherwise be adequately ministered to); he actively campaigned for the ordination of women as long ago as 1978; he appointed a lay parish worker to be in charge of a benefice. He developed the link between the diocese of Lincoln and the diocese of Brugge, finding a kindred spirit in Bishop de Smedt.

In other respects, he did not, I think, give a strong lead to the diocese and there were those who found this a real problem, but it was partly because he felt that people must be treated as adults and make their own decisions. He certainly felt deeply about the deprivation of many people in rural communities, and above all, he ruled out whole days in order to travel around that vast area, visiting the clergy and their families in their homes. Paying attention to them: a just and loving gaze directed upon those clergy and those families.

When Simon retired to Shipley in 1986 there began another, extremely fruitful stage, in his life and ministry. For one thing, he now had more time to paint, and he was an accomplished artist in oils. It involved, once more, attention – both to his own painting and to the great painters. Michael Mayne wrote: 'If you are going to let a painting speak to you, you have to respect its silence and its stillness. It has demanded an intensely concentrated act of seeing on the part of the artist and it isn't going to give up its secret at a hurried glance.'

For another thing, he gave himself up to friendship, a vast range of friendships formed over the years with every kind of person: princesses and psychotherapists, priests and politicians, hospital chaplains and the villagers of Shipley. There was huge affection for him here. But people would come from a distance to 'Sarsens' for his guidance and find themselves (we found ourselves) loved and accepted. He called us his *philadelphoi*, beloved brothers and sisters, and saw always the potential which was in us, what we might become. How typical of him to die at the very moment when he was speaking on the telephone to one friend and preparing supper for another! In many of us there is a tendency to be attention-seekers; Simon was an attention-*giver*.

My wife and I came back, just the other day, and stood once more in that familiar study. There was his chair, with the backrest (his back gave him a lot of trouble) and all around were piles of books, many of them new, many of them carefully read and marked up with a highlighter, books of theology, literature, biography, art criticism, photographs of Mary, paintings and Michelin maps of his beloved France. And that is where he prayed for us, seventeen whole pages of names remembered day by day as he said the morning Office.

That, in the end, is the key to the whole matter: Simon used to say that prayer is a giving of attention to what is the case:

namely that God *is* and that we *are*. Prayer is taking time to focus, to say 'Yes' to God, to open the channels of grace on behalf of X and Y and Z.

And here too in this church, on many Sunday mornings at 8 a.m. and on the day before he died, he led the people in giving their corporate attention to God, which is the inward and essential element in worship.

The truth is, of course, that all this is only our response, for God himself gazes on us with the creative eye of holy love. Simon used to say that he had an old American cousin who told him that when her husband proposed to her he said: 'I think you are about the most selfish person I have ever met, but you have possibilities.'

This is the great truth about us. None of us is just me as I am and that's that. There is always more in us to be discovered and explored and enjoyed and shared. That's how God sees us. It is the real self, with all its weakness, that he desires. He cannot transform us if we insist on only offering to him our goodness, our successes, our strengths. His gaze is transforming: he does not leave us in our poverty, but draws into being all we are meant to become.

Some of us saw Simon for the last time at the eucharist in Worth Abbey a fortnight ago. His own last words to us in this life were: 'The peace of the Lord be with you.'

Peace be with you, dear Simon.

Prayers of Thanksgiving at Simon Phipps's Memorial Service, written and read by Canon Stephen Roberts

Father, we thank you for all we received in knowing Simon.

For his marriage to Mary and all that together they enjoyed – for all that they gave of themselves, for their constancy, their gift of friendship and for the warmth of the welcome they extended to so many. *We pray for the relationships which nurture us, that they also may speak of a self-giving love.*

Lord hear us. Lord graciously hear us.

We remember Simon's skill and bravery as a soldier, and his self-effacing reluctance to talk about it. *We pray for all those who place themselves at risk by protecting liberty and who work for justice – that we may each grow in the courage we need to face what frightens or threatens us.*

Lord hear us. Lord graciously hear us.

We give thanks for Simon's ministry as a priest and bishop: for his flair as a college chaplain at Trinity, his commitment to industrial mission in Coventry, for the way he interpreted what it meant to be a bishop, in Horsham and Lincoln, for his truth-telling in being prepared to acknowledge what was hard for him, for his sense of fun and celebration – for the way shared laughter with him lit up your world, for his vision of the Kingdom and for his wish to break through false distinctions between what is sacred and what is secular. *We pray for the Church which Simon served, for all the different aspects of a lifetime's ministry represented amongst us – that we will be prepared to break new ground and see your grace at work through all that makes us human.*

Lord hear us. Lord graciously hear us.

'Prayer is attending to what is the case', he used to say. We give thanks for his seemingly endless willingness to listen, for the faithfulness of his intercessions and for the gentleness of his care. *May we not be too busy or driven that we speak when we need to listen, or plan when we need to pray.*

Lord hear us. Lord graciously hear us.

We give thanks for the way Simon rejoiced in the wonder of creation and sought to uncover and nurture what is beautiful: in his painting, through the changing seasons of the garden at 'Sarsens'; in his love for the villagers of Shipley and the worship at his parish church. *May we never ignore the sense of wonder, which is your gift to us, or overlook what we owe to our colleagues and neighbours.*

Lord hear us. Lord graciously hear us.

I have set before you life and death, blessing and curse; therefore choose life says Deuteronomy. We thank you for the countless ways Simon helped us to *choose life* and for the treasured memories he has left with us. *May we be faithful to his memory.*

Lord hear us. Lord graciously hear us.

O Thou who makest the stars, and turnest the shadow of death into the morning, we render thee, our Lord and King, the tribute of our praise; for the resurrection of the springtime, for the everlasting hopes that rise within the human heart, and for the gospel which has brought life and immortality to light. Receive our thanksgiving, reveal thy presence, and send forth into our hearts the Spirit of the risen Christ. Amen.

Sermon Preached in Southwark Cathedral by Simon Phipps on 25 April 1993, the 25th Anniversary of his Consecration there on St Mark's Day, 1968

Today is St Mark's Day, and I have always loved St Mark's Day, because I have always loved St Mark, and I will tell you why. It's because his gospel doesn't have an end. The last twelve verses of the gospel are clearly written in another hand. St Mark's bit ends in the middle of a sentence. Why, we don't know. Did he mean to end it like that, or was his end torn off and lost? Or because he was writing in the middle of the first persecution of the Christians in Rome, did he have to leave his manuscript there on the table and run for his life? Whatever happened, his gospel doesn't have an end. And I feel that that has an important message for us.

Because one of the important things about life, if we dare to face it, is that lots of things don't have an end. I say, 'if we dare to face it', because people rather like coming to conclusions about things; to get things buttoned up; don't like loose ends; what they call sometimes 'unfinished business'. But whether we like it or not, many of the most important things in life don't have an end. There is no end to the possibilities of life.

There is no end to the possibilities of each one of us: who we are, who we may become. It's all open-ended. If one is lucky enough to have someone in one's life one really loves, there is no end to love. You can't imagine saying, 'I now love you enough.' Perhaps more dauntingly, if we believe in God there is no end to his call upon us. 'Follow me' is Jesus's message to us. But of course, there is also no end to his offer to help us on the way.

This business of 'no end' is of course exciting, but it can be alarming too. There really is no end to many important aspects of life: it means that things will always be on the move, it means change, it means growth. And lots of people don't like all that. 'I know where I stand', people sometimes say. But standing hasn't much to do with 'Follow me'. Indeed, this is exactly why some people become religious. Religion can be a great and marvellous thing, but it can also go bad. And when it does, it can be turned into a wonderful way of staying put – wonderful because it's both comfortable and respectable.

I always think that there is a very sharp distinction between religion of this sort and faith. I see religion of this sort as having God on our terms, whereas faith is having God on God's terms. Having God on our terms as far as we dare, as far as we find manageable and convenient, as far as the points of risk and cost. And then we put an end to it. We draw the line. And I think all this goes to the heart of Christian faith, and to the heart of why the Church is not being more alive, more a live force in our world and in our time.

Because the heart of Christian faith is to do with what Jesus called the Kingdom. Jesus's teaching was all about the Kingdom. All those marvellous stories: the Kingdom is like this, the Kingdom is like that: always stories, stories, stories, because stories open up closed minds and open up closed hearts. Stories make you think and ask, 'What's he getting at?' 'I never thought of that.' 'Goodness! I see!' Stories open up vision, and then dear St Paul comes along – the first theologian. Of course he was a man of tremendous heart, as his marvellous chapter on love shows, and the many fascinating passages of autobiography in his letters. But with that he had this exceptional gift for turning it all into propositions. And on the whole the Church has tended to go along Paul's line of propositions about Christianity – 'This is what Christian faith means, this is the teaching of the Church, now get that into your heads!', instead of Jesus's line of stories, to make us think and feel for ourselves, think about Jesus, think about God, think about ourselves and about other people, think about life and about the endless possibilities of it all which are opened up for us by the best story of all: the story of Jesus's death and resurrection.

The resurrection tells us we can't put an end to things where God is concerned. The crucifixion shows us people trying to put an end to what they didn't like: to kill it off. The resurrection shows us that because God is, you can't put an end to things like that.

As quite an old man looking back on more than 40 years of ministry, and 25 years as a bishop – consecrated as a bishop by Michael Ramsey at that step there, 25 years ago today – I would say that the most important thing for the Church to do now is to renew its grasp of Jesus's idea of the Kingdom.

His idea of a Kingdom is something like this – that there is a potential in everything, everyone, every situation, every event, everything, which comes to the surface and becomes actual; actually emerges into our experience, as and when we live in a certain way. That way is the way of Jesus. And his way is the way of trusting God's call upon us all to live by love. When we do that, the Kingdom comes; things become as God made them to become. And we are not talking about something sentimental when we use the word 'love'.

For instance, as an industrial chaplain I know very well that when managements and trade unions have made arrangements for proper consultation by which they may really take each other's interest seriously – which is an example of love – things begin to work, possibilities build up, the factory becomes alive. So the Kingdom is always about the future, is always waiting to come, to be lived into and caught up in there ahead.

The Church is the community of people who believe God is calling them to work this out and live this out as servants of the Kingdom. So the Church is always a means to the end – which is the Kingdom – and never never never an end in itself. Because the Kingdom means living into a so-far-unknown future, Christians have tended to find it alarming. It doesn't submit to management and control, and so they have tended to live for the Church rather than for the Kingdom: to have the Church as an end in itself, an end to where there is no end.

The great failures of the Church in my time – its great timidity, as I see it – have been the result of this: the failure to unite with the Methodists, failure to make responsible adjust-ments to marriage discipline, almost failure to accept the ordination of women to priesthood. It is extraordinary to think that immediately after the war, with the nation being reconstructed all around, the Church spent so much of its energies on revising its own domestic rule-book – canon law – and it's interesting that it appointed as Archbishop[1] an administrator rather than a prophet. These sorts of failures reflect the failure to see the Church as a means to the Kingdom and a strong defensive propensity to see the Church as an end in itself.

And this tends to happen in the name of what people call, 'the Tradition' – what the Church carries through the ages. Of course the Church carries with it from the past all sorts of valuable things. I would call these 'traditions' and they are to be taken very seriously. But the Tradition is something quite different. The Tradition – what the Church carries out of the past into the present for the future, as the gospel, is what God has said to us in raising Jesus from the dead. And what the resurrection says to us is that God is to be trusted in calling us into the Kingdom, in spite of its costs and risks. So the Tradition of Christian faith is the cumulative experience of Christians through the ages, that God is to be trusted in calling us into his future, the future that is always there as a possibility in every new situation which life continuingly unfolds.

The gospel for St Mark's Day has in it the word 'end' three times – 'the end is still to come', 'before the end the gospel must be preached', 'the one who holds out to the end will be saved'. That is the only way Christians can use the word 'end' – that it is something which belongs to God and not to us, till, as today's epistle puts it, the whole thing grows and builds itself up in love – not so much the loving we do, as the infinite love that comes to us in proportion as we open our lives in trust to

---

1 Geoffrey Fisher.

God. That is our Faith. That is our Hope. That is the Love in which both are grounded. So may I ask you all to stand and to say with me the words of the *Gloria*, in the old traditional form: 'Glory be to the Father and to the Son and to the Holy Ghost, as it was in the beginning, is now and ever shall be, *world without end.* Amen.'